THE ADDICTION OF RELIGION

The Most Hated Book In America

K. D. Foy

Burning Desire Spiritual Recovery Services

ISBN-978-1-7356306-0-1 Paperback
ISBN-978-1-7356306-1-8 eBook
ISBN-978-1-7356306-2-5 Audiobook

Cover design by: K.D. Foy
Library of Congress Control Number: 2020917340
Printed in the United States of America

First and foremost, I dedicate this book to my soul. It was my soul's desire to share with the world these questions and ideas that will hopefully help you to discover truth and power.

I also dedicate this book to my beloved Mother Cora Walker, AKA my guardian angel, who passed away February 8th, 2008. She was the one who instilled within me so much life wisdom and the knowledge that I can make it on my own.

My son Jay is my heartbeat for because of him I desire to stay in this physical world.

My husband Byron has supported me in everything I have endeavored to dream and to be. Without his love and support, this book would not be possible.

To Jen Sincero who saved my life in 2015 with her book You are a Badass! I am now showing the world the Badass side of me!

To all of those who shared their personal stories, I thank you!

And finally, to the Universe in which all things are possible.

CONTENTS

INTRODUCTION

"True Religion is the life we lead, not the creed we profess."
Louis Nizer

I've been through a lot in my lifetime, but to be fair, who hasn't? I have come face to face and breath to breath with death more times in the last year than most people encounter in a lifetime. But I guess I should provide some color that will shed light on how I came to land at the crossroads that would determine if I remained in the land of the living or finally found out what truly happens in the afterlife up close and personally.

I guess one could say I was living a comfortable life compared to most, finally tipping six figures after 16 years on the job. I live in a loft downtown that could be in the movies in the Castleberry Hill loft district in Atlanta (they frequently film videos in our building and surrounding areas). Your girl only believes in having the best of everything! I have to have a 65-inch curved tv in my bedroom; I mean how else am I supposed to see the tv? I'm so cool that "I don't drive anymore." I had become so spoiled from having a driver take me everywhere in every country I visited for work that I now believed that being chauffeured should naturally continue at home. I had my dream job traveling the world, in business class, and Diamond Medallion- "Delta for life" thank you very much- running my little show. Since I couldn't possibly be seen in anything twice, that meant a trip shopping in whatever country I was working in to keep my wardrobe fresh. (Poor me, right?)

I can vividly remember when I accidentally got off the elevator on the secured fifth floor of my hotel in Mexico, where the President of Mexico was also staying. I came face to face with his armed guards with AK-47's, who didn't speak English but communicated to me that I must leave now! In one business dinner, I had seared duck, wild boar, escargot, venison, and crickets—yes black, hoppy crickets in the guacamole! I went shark swimming and island hopping in the Philippines. I traveled to live volcanos. I sweated my way through the infamous drug-infested customs in Bogota, Columbia. I prepped for meetings at the Hard Rock Café in Montego Bay, Jamaica.

I mean, I could go on and on, and all of this was for work! All of these things painted the glamorous picture that you could see from the outside, but on the inside, something else was brewing because suddenly, in just one day, it all came crashing down. In one moment, I lay not only physically dying, but my career was dying at the very same time.

In the boardroom, in the middle of my presentation, I collapsed. My blood pressure was plummeting. It had dropped to 60/40 when the paramedics arrived. I was slowly drifting into the peaceful oblivion of the great beyond (honestly, it was like falling into a deep, peaceful sleep). My coworker refused to let me go and strived with me to stay in this physical world. She said, "You will not die on me today!"

In two days, I was in three different hospitals in Guadalajara, Mexico. They rushed me from the plane to the final emergency room that would decisively determine that my body was nearly wholly dehydrated and that my body was shutting down from the strain of running on fumes. I was malnourished, dehydrated, and alcoholic. One drink at a time, I would pour the gas of alcohol that would fan the flames that consumed my body and soul to the brink of death.

Somehow, I missed all of the signs that I was an alcoholic. After all, I only drank to go to sleep, which caused me to wake to go to the bathroom (each time I had to drink myself back to sleep). Somehow in the days leading up to this final moment on the floor, I had missed all of the signs. Like when I almost got abducted by an overseas UBER driver who didn't speak English, but he did speak money, all of which I gave him as I cried and pleaded with him to return me to my hotel (while tearfully pushing his hand away as he tried to put it up under my dress!). Mind you; I came too in this UBER with no idea how I had gotten there. On another occasion, I was escorted by the police from an international airport when I "came to" and realized that after I passed out in the Delta Sky Club, I was too intoxicated to fly. I was humiliated and forced to stay in a dingy hotel near the airport to fly back to the U.S. the next day.

These are just a couple of my dirty little secrets that I hid from the world and even myself until it was almost too late. In the end, I was drinking the equivalent of a gallon of vodka per night to get to sleep and to stay asleep every single night. I planned my travel around where I could get my vodka in each country. If I traveled in the states, I had to locate the nearest liquor stores. After a couple of bad experiences, I learned to fly with a starter bottle in my luggage just in case I traveled on a Sunday, and the liquor stores were closed. I knew that all of the 7-11's sold alcohol overseas, but it was cash only in the currency of that country, so I always made sure to stop at the currency exchange at the airport after I landed. (Alcoholics are pretty smart!)

But getting back to the point, I barely made it home from Mexico. The flight nearly killed me as my blood pressure continued to plummet. During all of this, I had no idea that alcohol had anything to do with my condition. I would make it home only to get up close and personal with my local EMS at the fire station across the street because I would continue my trips to the E.R.

over the next month as my body fought to stay alive. I would come to my wit's end in the office of my psychiatrist, and in tears, I implored her to put me in a hospital so that I could get my body stabilized. I did not understand it at the time, but she would send me to a drug and alcohol rehab. She saved my life. And in the rehab, it would take another alcoholic to inform me of my alcoholism. Until that moment, I had no idea what was wrong with me. It was a crushing realization that the world that I fought so desperately to keep together was all a lie. The religion, my beliefs, and my whole way of thinking was only dust in my hands, which blew away in just one moment.

As a result of my journey through recovery, I have come to understand some fundamental truths through trial and error that have given me tremendous freedom. I have also learned that whenever ANYone says that ANYthing is the ONLY way to do ANYthing, I should probably run for the nearest exit. I also feel that it is pertinent to say that I am by NO means trying to convince anyone to follow me or dissuade anyone from their current belief system. This journey is for the hungry, the willing, and the ones seeking another way to understand their place in this vast universe. I never debate beliefs with anyone because I honestly believe that whatever religion you ascribe to is the right one if it fulfills your soul's desire to realize its highest self. But if you are reading this book, it might follow that there are unresolved areas of conviction within you that need to be satisfied. I am happy to share my experiences with you in this forum.

It takes a tremendous amount of arrogance to declare a definitive answer to almost anything in a vast universe that is so full of possibilities. For this reason, the years I spent as a consummate know-it-all leave me more than a bit embarrassed. In my defense, though, it's not all my fault. I believed a set of ideas and had to accept those ideas without speculation or close inspection of the validity of these notions. And to that point, what I find ironic, is that we were arrogant enough to casually dismiss any theology that did not support ours as pure lunacy and of the devil. Although, we made sure to display the appropriate amount of sympathy for their ignorance and to offer a prayer for the salvation of their heathenish souls.

This book, the result of my experiences and learning, explores religion from the viewpoint of religion as an unrecognized human addiction and is not for the faint of heart or resolute. It is not for the diehard theologian. It is not for the atheist. And it is not for the closed-minded. This book is for you if you think there is a God, but you are not sure what it means yet. It is for you if you feel that all of this religious stuff sounds mostly like bullshit and fairy tales. But you know there has got to be some point to all of this. It is for you if you are open to questioning everything you have ever learned, and you are not afraid to see what you might find out.

Throughout this book, I will reference different religious factions. There are too many to name. So to be fair, I will mix up the lists as I go. I neither mean any disrespect to any group nor absolve any group that I fail to mention within a particular reference. At the end of each chapter, I also include some perspectives on religion from individuals who were willing to share their points of view on the subject of religion. If you are not careful, you may find a perspective that resonates with your own.

The point is that there are no right or wrong ideas about religion. "God" (I use this term loosely) reveals itself to us through various life experiences. God will allow you to know it if you can accept the revelation. There are two ways to possess knowledge: intellectually and experientially. Having an experience is the only way to honestly "know" something. You may intellectually understand that fire is hot, but you do not know that fire is burning until you have been burned. In this book, you will find the revelations that I have come to experience. They have created my own "knowingness" about the truth of who and what God is.

I grew up in the "holiness church". To sum up the theology in short, in this religion, it is a sin to do almost anything fun! It is a sin for a woman to wear pants to watch tv, play sports, and wear makeup. You name it, it's probably a sin. Ha! Can you imagine growing up with the notion that hell was lurking behind every thought, action, or deed that created even a semblance of a good time that didn't include prayer and constant supplication to God? Then there was the fear that Jesus was "coming back." He's been coming back for the last 2000 years, but hell, today could just be the day. And if you weren't "ready", you would be left behind to suffer with all of humankind. "God" in His voyeuristic sadism, is always lurking and watching, ready to damn you to hell for even the slightest transgression.

I mean, think about it, you never really had a chance because ALL have sinned, and ALL of us were born into sin and shaped in iniquity. And if you're not "saved" from asking Jesus into your heart, then "Hell will be yo' po'tion" as so eloquently voiced by Evangelist Wilson. With those odds, why even bother to get out of bed in the morning? John the Revelator said only 144,000 people were going to make it in, so what's the point of living?

This type of thinking has served the most devout Christians around the world. Think about it. You have the Southern Baptists, the Amish, the Church of God in Christ, and let's not forget the likes of Jim Jones or the Branch Davidians. Somehow, we all bought into the idea that if we made one little mistake and died in that very moment without repenting, hell is your new home. At least the Catholics were smart enough to put in confession and those handy last rites to get forgiven even after you die. Nice touch, huh?

Maybe that's why they are the largest religion on the planet. You can do whatever the hell you want to do as long as you go and confess it to someone who is two to three times removed from God for forgiveness. Then you're alright! Statistics indicate over 70,000,000 million Catholics in the U.S. alone, so there MUST be something to their ideology.

You may not have been brought up in the strict denominations like I was, but most of us learned to believe in some "God" who lived only to punish us for the sins we committed daily. And we conveniently and fluidly devise whatever role or purpose we need God to serve for us at any given moment. And on the other hand, God was also your fairy God-father. You pray to Him for all the stuff you want or to get you out of that ticket you're about to receive for speeding. Surely, He should know that the only reason you were speeding is because you're about to be late for work. And, if you're late one more time, you are definitely getting written up this time. Oh, and I need to pass this test. And even though he drank himself to death, please don't let my dad die from cirrhosis of the liver.

God is also a fantastic scapegoat for all of the bad shit that happens to us! If there's a God, why are there starving people in Africa? Why did my husband leave me? How did He let that drunk driver kill my loved one? Basically, why does anything bad happen to anyone??? Then the pendulum swings to the opposite end of the spectrum with a God who is "Love". He loves everyone and everything, and He makes butterflies and faeries dance through the tulips. He is down for all the orgies of love-making your little heart can imagine. Anything goes, and drugs are the impetus to take this euphoria to the most spiritual place you can fathom. He's non-judgmental and open to it all. And if your tastes swing toward kids on the sexual revolutionary menu, well hell, it's all about love, right? And what could be wrong with that? And what of the aliens? Don't get me started on that one. We will talk about them a little later on in this journey.

Most of us have grown to believe in some version of this schizophrenic God and His intentions for all of us to live some sort of moral life. Right? And I was brought up in the strictest of religions, and even as a child, it didn't seem fair to me that others did not have to live the rigid lifestyle of the "saved." Why did those heathenish sinners get to have all of the fun??? As a result, my beliefs have morphed throughout the years from one extreme to another. In college, I took religious studies and found out that almost every religion around the world had some form of the creation story, flood story, holy man, or mythology. How could they all be wrong? Was it possible that they were all right? To make this all make sense, we have had to personify God.

Personification is the process by which we assign inanimate or inhuman things human qualities. So, in our search to understand our origin, we all seem to have decided to create a single (or in some cases multiple) God(s) that have the same human qualities, feelings, and emotions that we do. And we made Him or Her greater than ourselves, because well He'd have to be the creator, we gave Her the desire to punish and approve our behavior.

I am writing to understand myself and understand the effects that religion has had on my life. How could I—a fourth-generation Preacher's kid (PK), ordained Evangelist, two-time divorcee, international call center vendor manager making six figures per year—end up almost dead, clinging to life with a blood pressure of 60/40, and utterly humiliated on the conference room floor in Mexico? If God is real, how could my life end up this way?

The scripture chases, bible studies, revivals, and countless hours of church somehow failed me, and I ended up down the rabbit hole to reality so bizarre that even Alice in Wonderland would have to pause and say, "Girl, what the hell???". Whose fault is it that my universe collapsed so vehemently into rubble that I no longer recognized myself? And wait, it wasn't just me. I'm in great company. So many of the greats have had far worse ends than my own. Look at the most talented voice of all time, Ms. Whitney Houston. I just saw the life story of the Clark Sisters on Lifetime. OMG, I was shocked and appalled at how religion mishandled such delicate talent and anointing. The Grand Diva Tina Turner met with calamity the likes of no other with roots sown firmly in sacred soil. She found her escape through Buddhism. Is that the answer?

I am writing this book to chronicle my journey to answer the questions once and for all, who am I? Why am I here? What's my purpose? Who is God? What's the point of all of this? Some of the things that I discover are at the same time freeing, scary, disappointing, and simple. I want to lend my experience as a suggestion of the possibilities that exist for us all. I am here to simply pose the question, "What if?" And if something that I write resonates with you in some meaningful way, then maybe YOU are helping me fulfill my purpose. Wouldn't that be amazing? What if I get to be Jesus, Buddha, or Tao De Ching for you and be your great bringer of truth with this book? It's possible, right? Because anything is possible in this vast universe.

You will note that a quote about religion prefaces each chapter. The quotes come from various backgrounds and points of view. I do not necessarily agree with, stand behind, or support ANY or ALL of these quotes. These quotes are representative of various standpoints about religion or maybe a particular chapter in this book. The purpose of these quotations is to create a dialogue or to cause you to ponder its validity. Remember, this book is to challenge you to examine other vantage points that may differ from your own. For far too long, we have accepted others' beliefs as truth without even questioning an opposing outlook. For some, it feels uncomfortable. But I encourage you to explore this discomfort because, through it, you will create your own experience with truth to self.

"Truth learned can be questioned, but truth experienced cannot be denied." K. D. Foy

So, I welcome you to put all of your preconceived notions about religion aside and consider how we all fell into this addiction called religion. Let's see how it happened, why it happened, and what we can do about it. I know it's scary. No one wants to know how hot dogs are made. (insert chuckle here) But there are so many misconceptions that, in reality, neither work for us nor serve us. Let's stop playing the game. Let's unshackle ourselves from these chains and find the serenity and freedom we so desperately seek in understanding our higher power and our highest self.

I feel like I have to mention that I am by no means bashing religion. I have the utmost respect for all beliefs. I am open to everything and attached to nothing, as Wayne Dyer would so eloquently phrase it. However, I am taking a hard-long look at the possibility that religion has failed us in many ways, as with all of man's attempts at systems for governing people. For example, look at the prison system. Do prisons deter crime in any way, shape, or form? America is the land of the free but has the highest rate of imprisoned population in the world.

And what of the public-school system? The dropout and pregnancy rate of youth is astronomical. The welfare system has become a generational sinkhole for failure, a far cry from the temporary economic reprieve it should offer. Healthcare, politics, government, and so many other diasporas that I could mention further laud man's undeniable failure to its kind to create systems for harmonious living. Yet, it is taboo to examine the insolvencies created by religion. And still, we cling to its stories and promises for dear life and dare not question or speak an ill word against its heartiness. Oddly, it's entirely acceptable to denigrate opposing religions that dare defy the authority of our own.

I, in no way, presume to have all of the answers. During this read, you may find that perhaps I ask more questions than I supply definitive answers. But isn't that the point? Question everything and believe nothing until you have the experience that reveals to you YOUR truth unequivocally. Only then can you have the answers that you seek, not from religion but from within yourself. You will also find that I refer to God by several names and sexes. You cannot limit God, so I may suggest that God is He, Her, or It. Do not be confused by the term Universal Source Energy or Consciousness. These are all God who has no name that you can name.

The effects of religion upon each of us is such a unique and personal experience for each individual. At the end of each chapter, a particular person I have encountered will share their perspective on how religion has touched their lives. Each account had no guidance or instruction on what to write (except for the subject matter) not to influence their experience or impact their opinion in any way. Perhaps, one of these experiences will resonate with your own. We shall see. There are also pre-prescribed debate questions that are there to challenge your beliefs. But if you are reading this book, the universe has guided you to look for answers. And if you are fearless, I encourage you to use the debate questions to spark a dialogue with others to push the limit of what feels right for you.

PART ONE: THE ADDICTION

CHAPTER 1 A GLIMPSE AT THE HISTORY OF RELIGION

"True religion is not about possessing the truth. No religion does that. It is rather an invitation into a journey that leads one toward the mystery of God. Idolatry is religion pretending it has all the answers." John Shelby Spong

Okay, so they say it's impolite to talk about politics, religion, and money. Well, two out three ain't bad! We have to discuss religion candidly if we want to stay abreast of all of the rapidly occurring changes in our society. Religion is one subject that touches 100% of our lives worldwide in one way or another. Whether it is the religious symbols or words on our dollar bills or the questions around the separation of church and state, we are affected. Nothing has created more controversy and fueled more wars, both holy and otherwise, than religion. The subject of religion can raise ire in people that will emotionally infuriate them to the point of violence in defense of their religious beliefs.

The abortion issue is a subject of debate with religious edicts of morality at the crux of the pro-life movement. We no longer "swear to tell the truth, the whole truth, so help me God" on the bible in our courtrooms. If you don't believe in Jesus Christ as your Lord and Savior, you will burn in hell. A tiny faction claims not to know if there is a God, but if you pressed them, they would admit that they believe that there must be something out there running all of this.

Whether you choose aliens and UFO's or 1000 different demi-gods, we almost all believe in something greater than ourselves. Our belief is because there is an innate desire to understand who we are and where we originate. It seems to be in our DNA in code of some kind to seek out a creator. After all, we are all creators ourselves, and we must have gotten this tendency from somewhere. So, for most, we seek the answers to these questions in the form of religion.

Webster defines religion as a set or system of religious attitudes, beliefs, and ways of doing things. It also defines addiction as a compulsive, chronic, physiological, or psychological need for a habit-forming substance, behavior, or activity having harmful physical, mental, or social effects and typically causing well-defined symptoms (such as anxiety, irritability, tremors, or nausea) upon withdrawal or abstinence. Can you be addicted to religion? If so, then the question becomes, *Is faith perfect for me?* Or *What is the point of religion if it doesn't provide the comfort and security that it promises?*

One of the most paraphrased beliefs of Karl Marx is that religion is the opiate of the masses. Karl Marx argues that religion plays a significant role in maintaining the status quo by promising rewards in the afterlife rather than in this life. He supported the abolition of religion as the illusory happiness of the people. I tend to agree with Marx that religion serves to maintain the status quo. By focusing attention on otherworldly rewards, religion pacifies members by providing a worldview that deflects attention that would otherwise look at the inequalities of this world. Faith, Marx held, was a significant hindrance to reason, merely masking the truth and misguiding followers. Are we addicted to religion? Are we easily manipulated by the guidance and instructions for living that religion provides? Are we addicted to being right? Are we addicted to allowing others to think for us? Are we addicted to the answers, the promises, and the hope that religion offers? Did Karl Marx get it right?

There is a solution for every problem or at least a reason that we can manipulate religion to rationalize or explain easily. Spirituality provides a rationale for Aids, COVID-19, hurricanes, earthquakes, and forest fires and tells us that they are all communications from God expressing His or Her displeasure with our behavior. We can earmark every adverse event as a cryptic message from God to reinforce our religious agenda. David Koresh did this very well to the demise of himself and his followers.

One could argue that religion provides a ready explanation or excuse to justify every situation that we encounter. And if we twist the words appropriately enough, we can also provide validation and justification for our behaviors. Even racists are justified and filled with righteous indignation. But we will look at them a little later on in our journey.

Many of us who fall into drug, alcohol, food, sex, gambling, or any other form of addiction can identify with a lack of identity with who we are as related to God and religion. This addiction to religion and the results of the failures found in the premises of faith that do not support us in a healthy way of living creates a quagmire of empty spaces and voids that we use our traditional addictions to fill. That was a lot of words, so let me break it down. Questions of sexual identity, sexual violations in our early years, lack of family support and structure, painful loss, hurts obtained from members of the clergy, and depression has roots that may point to the disconnect found within our spiritual lives.

The controversial 11th step of AA suggests, "Sought through prayer and meditation to improve our conscious contact with God as we understood Him, praying only for knowledge of His will for us and the power to carry that out." They believe that prayer and meditation are our principal means of conscious contact with God. It would follow that without this contact, one's sobriety is in jeopardy. I can't argue against this suggestion, but I am cautious about how I interpret it.

"You don't drown from falling in the water; you drown by staying there." Edwin Louis Cole

To explore this foundation, we have to take a candid look at religion and how it came to be an integral part of our lives worldwide. Let's start by exploring the five significant beliefs, their premises, and the values they purport to be true. I in no way wish to disparage, belittle, or oversimplify any religion's fundamental nature in this book. It is merely my aspiration to shed light on the various positions that religions take on how we should live in our diverse cultures. This book is only a taste of the possibilities that each religion offers so that you can understand a little bit of how the other world lives in relationship to your way of living. You may be surprised at how similar or how different your belief system is from some of the other frames of reference.

"How thoughtful of God to arrange matters so that, wherever you happen to be born, the local religion always turns out to be the true one." Richard Dawkins Hinduism

Hinduism

Hinduism, the 3rd largest religion globally, is claimed to be the world's oldest religion. Roughly 95% of its followers are from India. And while it is not known to have a specific founder, it is purported to be a cornucopia of philosophies and traditions. Hinduism revolves around two principal doctrines: 1. That all life follows karma, the universal law of cause and effect, and 2. Samsara represents the continuous cycle of life, then death, then reincarnation. Hindus believe as henotheistic people in the God Brahman, but also acknowledges a myriad of other gods and goddesses. My favorite modern-day proclaimed Hindu goddess is the lovely Jyoti Amge, aka "Ma Petite" from one of my favorite series known as American Horror Story. She is named the smallest woman in the world at a mere 23" tall. Many in India consider her to be the incarnation of a goddess because of her short stature.

Atman, or the belief in man's soul as a derivative of the supreme soul, is at the cornerstone of this ideology. Moksha, or salvation, is man's ultimate goal, which will end the cycle of reincarnation and ultimately cause the soul to join the absolute soul. The law of karma suggests that one's action directly impacts both your current and future lives. So, the objective of life is to strive for dharma, the right way of life, and conduct. I won't bog you down with the particulars of Hinduism, although I strongly suggest you explore its history and philosophy more intensely if your curiosity is aroused. The main points that I want to highlight are the ideas of "salvation" and reincarnation until moksha. Hinduism seems to suggest that man is imperfect at birth and must amend his living in such a way to achieve worthiness to gain release from the cycle of life.

Buddhism

Buddhism grew out of Hinduism, but unlike Hinduism's evolutionary characteristics, Buddhism was founded by "The Buddha" Siddhartha Guatama, more than 2,500 years ago in India. Buddhists reject the idea of a God or supreme deity (Except for Buddha himself...chuckle.) However, they do hold that life has a singular purpose, and that is to achieve enlightenment, which is a state of inner peace and wisdom. The end game is to, at some point, achieve Nirvana, which is the highest spiritual echelon one can attain. Like Hinduism, they embrace the ideas of reincarnation and karma, and the main two pillars of theology are the Four Noble Truths and the Eightfold Path. The Four Noble Truths are:

1. The truth of suffering (Dukkha)
2. The truth of the cause of suffering (Samudaya)
3. The truth of the end of suffering (Nirhodha)
4. The truth of the path that frees us from suffering (Magga)

By Buddhist philosophy, the path that frees us from suffering is to follow the Eightfold Path of ethical conduct, wise living, and discipline: Right understanding, thought, speech, action, livelihood, effort, mindfulness, and concentration. Like Christianity and Judaism, Buddhism has its own set of holy books called the Book of the dead, Sutras, and Tipitaka. Again, the theory of "right living" suggests that man is born in a state of moral imperfection and can only become perfected or enlightened by living his or her life in an ethical way of life.

I feel the need to mention that I find many of the suggestions within the Buddhist principles, such as the art of meditation, to be excellent practices that would aid in living the life of your best self if one chose to incorporate them. However, the conception that all of life comes from suffering does not ring true for me personally. Much of our activity in life at a base level is the avoidance of pain. But in my mind, these actions support self-preservation and are not necessarily the point of your existence. Suffering is subjective, and it is, therefore, reckless to attribute pain to everyone.

Judaism

On the other hand, Judaism is an Abrahamic faith whose foundation is rooted in the existence of the one true God of Abraham. Judaism is characterized by a belief in one transcendent God who revealed himself to Abraham, Moses, and the Hebrew prophets. It teaches a religious life based on the scriptures and rabbinic traditions. You could argue that this religion is highly exclusive. The Jews are proclaimed by their faith to be the chosen people of God and to exist in a covenantal relationship with Him. They have their books of holy writings that document their history and their relationship with God. Not only is the Tenakh believed to be an ancient text written over 1000 years ago, but it also includes the Torah and other sacred writings by the prophets, poems, prophecies, and hymns that encompass the whole history of the world from the moment of creation.

Familiar to most are the laws given to Moses on Mt. Sinai, which are called the Torah and include the ten commandments. These laws are to be God's instruction to govern daily life. The Talmud is a collection of Jewish writings by the rabbis over 2000 years ago, explaining how to implement the Torah in everyday living. What marks Judaism as unique for me is the strictness of the guidelines that God gave them to live their lives from what to eat, who to marry, the transition to adulthood, etc. So, for this reason, I have to acknowledge Judaism as more than just a religion; it is a way of life.

In their opinion, God provided lengthy and detailed instructions for this chosen group on morality, ceremony, and right living. For example, there are many rituals and observations that they must follow, which they have observed for millennia. From sundown on Friday evening until sunset on Saturday evening is considered the Sabbath and must be kept holy in observance of God's day of rest on the seventh day of creation. They only eat kosher foods (among other dietary restrictions), a unique way of preparing meats for consumption. The most crucial detail that I will mention about Judaism is the fact that this religion belongs primarily to members of Jewish descent. So, if you were not born Jewish, this is probably not the religion to pursue. Although in all fairness, conversion to Judaism is a possibility for any who are serious enough to continue the vigorous study of learning the Hebrew language and the lifestyle adjustments.

Christianity

Christianity grew out of Judaism and is the most popular religion in the world. Christianity rests upon the premise that as prophesied in the old testament, a savior would come to save God's people. When Jesus Christ lived, died, and rose again from the grave, his resurrection would be the manifestation of that promise. He was the fulfillment of God's pledge to send a healer, deliverer, and savior of the Jewish people as fulfilled by his death, burial, and resurrection. His ultimate ascension would follow his resurrection to heaven.

For the Jews, Judaism was God's law until the savior would come, and the law would be replaced by accepting Jesus Christ into your heart. Sacrifices for sin would cease as Jesus' sacrifice by dying on the cross would be the last and final sacrifice. His blood at the crucifixion would be the blood that will cover all of our sins. He summed up the law and the commandments with two new commandments: "Thou shalt love the Lord thy God with all thy heart, and with all they soul, and with all thy mind." And "Thou shalt love thy neighbor as thyself."

His second request was the following: "And he said unto them, Go ye into all the world, and preach the gospel to every creature." He also mandated the practice of communion, which served as a remembrance of Him in Mark 14:22-24. Here he stated that his blood indicated the new covenant, and the wine would represent his blood, and the bread represents his body. With this said, much of the other doctrine and edicts that self-proclaimed Christian groups have incorporated into their teachings in the name of Jesus is astounding! There are issues about morality, sexual relations, sexual orientation, gender roles, just to name a few, that are engineered, exaggerated, or taken out of historical context to justify their agendas.

Much of the ideology comes from writings written after Jesus' death by his disciples. Most of which is primarily written by The Apostle Paul, who never even met Jesus. He penned 13-14 out of the 27 books of the new testament. These books were a compilation of letters that he sent to various churches established in the early days of Christianity. There were apparent variations on how they would conduct themselves, and the new Christians adopted many of the beliefs associated with their geographical locations. I would like to point out that not only did Paul never even meet Jesus, but his writings provide much of the church doctrine that we hear in churches today.

Jews who were followers of Christ are called Christians, and they followed the teachings of Jesus. King James and his team chose to include the contents of the Torah and the Old Testament writings with the new testament in the bible. As a rule, animal sacrifice should have been done away with after the resurrection since Jesus was to be the final sacrifice. Most churches choose to keep the concept of tithing and offerings conveniently, which by today's standards, tithes and offerings denote giving 10% of your income to the church and monies that are requested from the constituents as the church sees fit. Ironically, the original purpose of tithing was to provide food for the priests, infirmed, orphans, and widows who were in need. Tithes are not to help churches get more prominent buildings, airplanes, or fancy cars for religious leaders.

The most challenging issue I have pondered in my journey in Christianity, which means Christ-like, is the dichotomy between today's Christian and one who is Christ-like. Jesus was nonjudgmental, accepting of everyone, and tolerant of individual perspectives. His message was one of love and tolerance. He fed the hungry, healed the sick, and taught a message of love and kindness to your fellow man. Jesus never judged anyone harshly, and, on many occasions, he forgave the people who were sinners and advised them to sin no more.

He forgave the woman at the well who was a prostitute and defended the woman caught in the act of adultery by telling the men who wanted to stone her, "Let he who is without sin, cast the first stone" in John 8:7. Jesus even told us that people would know that you were a Christian by the love that you show one another, John 13:35. For this reason, I can appreciate much of what Jesus taught his followers. Sadly, his behaviors are not what I see demonstrated by so-called Christians today in many instances. More often than not, the term Christianity serves as a cloak of identity in principle rather than indeed.

Islam

According to history, Islam, the second-largest religion in the world, began circa 1400 years ago by the prophet Muhammad who was visited by the angel Gabriel. Gabriel imparted to him the word of Allah over several years. The flawless, immutable, and final revelation word of Allah is recorded in the Quran. In addition to the prophet Muhammad, Adam, Abraham, Moses, and Jesus are great prophets. The Five Pillars of Islam are their guide to right living. They encourage Muslims to pray five times a day, fast during Ramadan, the pilgrimage to Mecca, declare "There is no god but God, and Muhammad is his prophet," and pay money to the poor.

Muslims assert that they believe in the same God as the Judeo-Christian religions. However, they do not believe in God's holy trinity, the Father, the Son, and the Holy Spirit. To do so would be considered as polytheism. It was quite impressive how much scripture of the Koran and the bible is similar. The Koran has many of the same stories of the bible's old testament. But how is it that while serving the same God, the messages from God are so very different in many ways.

Islamic principles include the belief in an afterlife that suggests a continued existence for the human soul in a transformed physical body that you will continue into either paradise or hell. Where you spend eternity depends on your life's actions as reviewed by God on the day of judgment--the last day where the world is destroyed. For this reason, radical Muslims commit the holy act of Jihad (which means struggle or effort) or holy war against those that the Muslims perceive to be enemies of their faith. They believe that they will receive a reward in heaven replete with virgins to please them throughout eternity for their efforts. Christianity has similar views about a judgment day, as detailed in the book of The Revelation in the bible. So, we see yet again that righteous living is the expectation from God because on that last day, if your good deeds do not outweigh your evil deeds, you will spend eternity in hell.

What Can We Surmise From All Of This

These main five long-established religions by no means represent all of the variations of religious philosophies that exist in the world today. They are, however, the most widely embraced and followed by the masses worldwide. In this writing, we will look at additional religious convictions in later chapters. But what we can surmise from each religion in this chapter suggests that each religion requires the believer to live a moral life as defined by its holy writings. And while the backstories for each religion are different, they all share a familiar theme—We cannot live life the way that we want to live it. We must follow these rules as outlined by either God or divinely inspired religious leaders.

Following one or more of these religious paths has shaped many negative experiences for some of its struggling followers. I've met too many people who have been "hurt by the church" (myself included). How many children have fallen prey to a pedophile in cleric's clothing? Who hasn't heard of a preacher who hasn't fallen from grace into the lustful bosom of a beautiful woman who wasn't his wife? Who hasn't been promised a miracle or blessings for the small donation of $____? Ever see the "good reverend" take a sip or a puff when he thought no one was looking? Still, the religious machine rages on as usual. Did God create two people, put them in paradise, allow them to make one mistake, and doom all the rest of humanity to hell? Does God care if I tell a little white lie? The questions could go on forever; still, 80% of Americans believe in God in this religious sense.

Some people feel that the stories in the many holy books, such as the flood story or the creation stories, wreak of the fables of folklore and mythology, yet we believe them. In my opinion, it would be wise to take a broader approach to read these writings. Much of the original meaning is lost in translation, personal translator bias, and historical influence. It is probably illogical to adhere to a literal interpretation of these ancient writings. But it can be helpful to consider the essence and overarching ideas of holy texts and internalize the pieces of scripture that we can realistically incorporate into living in today's world.

You may chuckle about our children believing in Santa Claus and the Easter bunny. You may sternly promote the snake's story in the garden, tricking people into eating apples as gospel truth. But is it within the realm of possibility that Allah, God, and Jehovah are all the same and that neither is real? Is it plausible that Muhammad and Moses received similar or the very same message from God, and they are both equally inaccurate? Or could it be that one or more of these ancient religions plagiarized the other? And what of the Book of Mormon? It gives an account of Jesus here in America. Are we to believe that Jesus beat even Christopher Columbus to the punch and discovered America?

I wasn't there, so, within the universe, such a reality must exist somewhere. But why do we feel lost if we don't have someone to pray to in troubled times? And if you never read a book, never went to church, or never met another soul, what would you believe? Would there still be a God? If I woke up from a coma with amnesia, would I feel the need to pray? How you choose to view God is the result of what someone else has influenced you to believe. I have met people who have an almost real aversion to any argument that might hint that their beliefs are less than accurate. Or they squirm when asked for a logical explanation for one of the principles or stories in the bible that do not make sense. It's interesting that even though they can't explain it either, the go-to response is almost to say "Because I said so" or "Because the bible said so" as if shooing away a petulant child for asking too many questions. Or, "just have faith because we will understand it better by and by."

We also draw conclusions and assumptions about the events in our lives that we experience and shape them to support our religion's premises so that our doctrine will conveniently fit into the situations we incur. Both God and the Devil are blamed interchangeably for things that they would have no interest in whatsoever if you were able to ask them. However, when something does not fit into the illusion of how we view God's purpose in our lives, we are sorely disappointed. We look to blame God (or the Devil for that matter) for not fulfilling our illusory perception of the role that either entity might fulfill in our lives.

For example, surely it was God that helped me to get that promotion. But where was God when my loved one didn't recover from surgery? The serial killer attacked someone in my area; he is evil for what he did to those innocent people. We have to have a way to explain all of these things. We all need to reconcile the good and the bad things that happen in the world so that it all fits neatly in a little basket. The problem is that the basket isn't always quite so neat. And yet we hold on relentlessly with hope against hope. Thus, the question is—is it all just an addiction?

Next Steps and Takeaways from this Chapter:

The Debate: For all of their similarities, is it possible that all of these religions are correct? Or could they be all wrong?

It is always good to investigate the history behind whatever religious point of view you have decided to make your own. If you are a Jehovah's witness, which is a derivative of Judaism, research the origin of the Jehovah's witnesses. Read outside perspectives on Jehovah's Witnesses. Don't just absorb the literature that is provided by your church. If this religion is a spinoff of another, why the separation? What was wrong with the original religion? I would recommend that you write down all of the things that you have questions about in your mind.

You know, those ideas that don't quite make sense to you. Like why can't we celebrate holidays? Why would God care one way or the other?

For example, I always wondered if God knows everything, wouldn't He already know that man would eat the forbidden fruit? And if He knew and only wanted to give them a choice to obey or disobey, why didn't He scrap them and start over when they failed the test? Why would He allow EVERYONE ever born for eternity to be doomed to hell? There is no scenario or answer to this question that would make any sense to me, yet it is precisely this kind of problem that is usually swept under the rug to be addressed by the catchall of "just have faith." I recommend to everyone that I do personal recovery work to face these kinds of questions. If they are ultimately dissatisfied with the answer or lack of explanation, this is a legitimate cause to abandon the idea as truth.

It is okay not to know the answer, but to accept an answer on blind faith will stunt your ability to receive or eventually find out the truth. Likewise, when you scrutinize your religious life as a practice, examine the root cause for your participation. Is your involvement out of fear of hell or some other adverse outcome if you don't comply? Are you reliant upon your social standing within your organization for support or validation? Are you participating in some sense of obligation to family or others who have provided care for you? Have you continued to blindly remain "faithful to your faith" despite nagging moments of doubt just to belong?

To sum things up, let's mull over a few basic questions. Are you sticking with what you believe because you haven't found a suitable alternative? Have you found yourself seeking out religion after religion for answers? If so, this is a glaring red flag. It would indicate that your faith is not truly your truth. You may have switched because your original belief system was flawed. You may have coupled with someone of a different faith. Either way, if you turned from a religion that you have deemed a defective system, chances are very high that there is a flaw in your new system as well if you are completely honest with yourself. Be sure that you do not tend to ignore these glaring inconsistencies to belong.

Meet Ashley in her own words:

Growing up, I was raised in the church. Every Sunday morning, at 11 am service, I was with my mom, dad, and sisters. If not with the main church body, I was in Sunday school. The church life was great. I even joined the children's choir, which requires Wednesday and Saturday practices. Every holiday had some time of church involvement. Easter was a fashion show. Halloween was to pray off the evil spirits. Christmas was to celebrate the birth of Jesus Christ. The church was my first real experience being social outside of school. I've overcome a lot of my shyness by singing in front of an entire church body while being on the choir. I loved my little church environment. I learned all of the popular church songs that I still sing today.

My favorite memories of my sister are laughing at her for being yelled at for falling asleep during the sermon. My church had a family feeling; everyone knew everyone, ate together and took out of town trips together. I appreciated this interaction because all I had here was my small immediate family. I was nervous, excited, and proud to be baptized in front of my church family.

Over time our space became too small to fit all the members comfortably. A bigger and better church sounded like a dream, but little did I know; this would affect my small church family environment. When we moved to the new bigger church, everything felt and looked like the churches in movies. Big colossal tv screens, excellent surround sound systems, a balcony pew, a quiet room for the babies to not disturb the main church. Unfortunately, with a bigger church came a bigger ego and the greed of money. My little church had the dream to be a massive church like you see on tv.

The first change I didn't like was the matching robes of the pastors and choir. It felt very cult-like to me. I had one distinct memory that turned me away from my church forever. On the tv screens were the big letters to collect the offering. Collecting offering is always normal because the church has bills to pay. I remember at my small church, there were two offering collections. Once at the beginning of service, and one near the end of service to catch those who may have come in late. This time was different. There was an image that seemed to condemn anyone who did not pay their offering on the TV screen. The pastor would say a sermon to condemn you for not paying for the offering. It seemed like spotlights and eyes were on you if you didn't put anything in the basket. This experience happened four times during that sermon. As a child, I felt like my church bit more than they could chew for this new church's expenses.

I remember (I) dreaded going to church. Our every Sunday 11 am service turned into well... let's at least go 1st and 3rd Sunday. This turned into let's just go to the 1st Sunday service early in the morning so we can get out quicker. Next was okay; let's just make sure we go on the holidays. Eventually, that ended too, and now 13 odd years later, I haven't stepped into a church again. My church-going days is a distant childhood memory.

As an adult, I sometimes want to be a part of a church family again, but I crave the small intimate family feeling churches. The greed and business feeling of mega-churches have deterred me from going back to church.

CHAPTER 2 THE AGE OF PAZUZU: SATANISM, WITCHCRAFT, AND OTHER ALTERNATIVE RELIGIONS

> *"On Saturday night, I would see men lusting after half-naked girls dancing at the carnival, and on Sunday morning when I was playing organ for tent-show evangelists at the other end of the carnival lot, I would see these same men sitting in the pews with their wives and children, asking God to forgive them and purge them of carnal desires. And the next Saturday, they'd be back at the carnival or some other place of indulgence. I knew then that the Christian church thrives on hypocrisy, and that man's carnal nature will out no matter how much it is purged or scoured by any white-light religion."*
> *Anton LaVey*

Although religion has a long history in man's civilization, there have also existed the antagonists of religion (anti-religions if you will.) What is poignant to me is that these factions are not anti-religious at all but in themselves, religions that represent philosophies that are sometimes opposed to typical religious organizations. Some look to the stars for answers. But either way, I invite you to take a peek with me into the views of some trains of thought of what one might consider being the darker religions. I won't tell you with which ones, but I have found some of their ideas exciting or even to mirror my thoughts on some points. And in the vein of keeping an open mind, ponder how your own beliefs may differ, resound, or intertwine, (even if in secret), with these religions. I cannot list every single alternative religion, but I did try to mention the most well-known and widely followed dogmata and creeds. I love how diverse the universe is that so many variations of belief coexist in the world. If the possibilities are endless, why shouldn't the number of religions be infinite? Whether I agree or not with these concepts is not my place to say. But every possibility of belief exists to be explored, and that is precisely what we will do here.

Satanism

Although paganism has a history steeped and embedded throughout man's history, an official Satanic church as a recognized religion was founded some 50 years ago by Anton LaVey. The idea of Satan or Lucifer, the fallen angel, has its origins in religious scripture. Lucifer is said to be the most beautiful angel (the angel of light), and he was God's chief angel and right hand. He later becomes an anti-hero of sorts, the villain who fights against the right side of God. Other religions have a similar manifestation of "The Devil" within their religious frameworks. In Buddhism, Maara represents the Devil as one who tempted Buddha away from his path to enlightenment. In Islam, Shayton mainly shares the same story as the Christian version of Lucifer, the chief angel, who essentially rebelled against God in heaven. Typically, in most of these viewpoints, the Devil is defeated by the representative of good in the end. The constant struggle of good versus Devil presents the dichotomy of man's innate struggle to either be morally right or immorally evil.

For many of our disenfranchised youth, Satanism is the "bestest", "coolest" fantasy land to play God, the Devil, and lusty angels both simultaneously and interchangeably. Many of these youth come from broken homes, are victims of sexual violation, and have histories of both addiction and physical abuse. I can see the appeal of having dark powers and a sense of control over others. There is the draw of freedom and ecstasy in giving oneself entirely over to his base needs, wants, and desires in wanton abandon. The element of defiance against all of the authorities that strangled away your sense of self could be seductive. Even though LaVey intended to create some sense of order and structure to legitimize Satanism as a distinct religion, there are no rules. And that's the point, Satanism, without the proper intended "guidance," gives its followers permission to indulge in anti-society, immoral behavior without the system of checks and balances that traditional religion provides. Herein lies the danger.

Pazuzu

On October 28th, 2015, Pazuzu Illah Alagarad was found dead in a pool of blood on a bed in his cell after a presumed suicide. His death occurred after nearly one year of his incarceration in jail for the murder of three people. He committed the murders with the participation of his associates. He is demonized by some and worshipped by others for his staunch belief and practice of the dark arts of Satanism, an anti-God interpretation of religion. His story is relevant because so many of today's youth are searching for answers that will point them to a sense of identity and connection to some form of religion. His saga further reflects how far individuals who share these beliefs in Satan will demonstrate their allegiance to their cause. Which begs the question, why is the addiction of religion so powerful and all-consuming that even the darkest and dangerous form of religious expression becomes appealing? Pazuzu had many followers, including a girlfriend who willingly participated in sexual orgies, drug use, and the deadliest crime of murder in what felt like for them total obedience to God's will.

Aleister Crowley

They told me that I absolutely could not complete this section without at least an honorable mention of Aleister Crowley. He is relevant to this chapter specifically because he had very few followers in life, so he neither meets the criteria of religion nor a cult per se. However, in death, he became a cult figure in pop culture for all things evil. The Beatles put his picture on the Sgt. Pepper's Lonely Heart Club Band album cover. Led Zeppelin guitarist Jimmy Page purchased a house previously owned by Crowley near Loch Ness in Scotland. He even designed his version of Tarot Cards, which are still in use to this day. His interpretation of the cards, as written in The Book of Thoth, currently has a 4.1 out of 5-star rating. They laud the deck as one of the best companions to the Tarot deck.

He was dubbed as a Satanist by the press, and he Is an early representation of an antithesis to conventional religion. They note him as an Occultist poet, mountaineer, and novelist. However, his beliefs and practices earned him the title of "the wickedest man in the world." This title is after the mysterious death of one of his followers as a result of his sacrilegious rituals. He was a sadist, bisexual, and practitioner of sex magic. He christened himself the prophet of Thelema, his religion, and wrote The Book of the Law, which embodies the ideology "Do what thou wilt shall be the whole of the law." This commandment was allegedly given to him in Egypt by the Islamic god Alwass the messenger of Horus. Aleister liked to refer to himself as the Beast 666 and also Ipssissimus- beyond the gods. He expressed his perceived blasphemy against Christianity and the bible. Ironically, his father was a Christian evangelist, and the greatest irony of all is, despite his majesty, he died a penniless heroin addict in a rooming house in 1947.

Scientology

Scientologists neither ascribe to the idea of a monotheistic God per se nor focus on the mind and body. They believe in the development of the spirit. Developed by L. Ron Hubbard, Scientology is a religion that offers a spirituality-based pathway that will ultimately lead its followers to a complete and specific understanding of one's true spiritual nature. Scientology also addresses your relationships to yourself, your family, to your fellow man, to all life forms, the material and spiritual universes, and the Supreme Being. And if your beliefs tend to lean toward the presence of aliens and extraterrestrial influencing upon our world and science fiction dogma, there is plenty to wet your whistle here.

It's all fascinating because they believe that ancient beings from a distant intergalactic civilization contained millions of creatures. After the destruction of their galaxy, these beings called "body thetans" came to Earth to parasitically latch on to the spirits of human beings. This attachment produces intense trauma to the human host's spirit in both their current and past lives. These attachments are the cause of all of the problems of the human condition. They believe that humans are immortal beings called thetans. The only way to attain relief from these oppressors is through a process called auditing. The process involves a device called E-meter, which Scientologists say measures the body's electric flow as an auditor asks a series of questions, they say, reveals sources of trauma. These questions help you identify the causes of your distress and thus implement the appropriate Scientology tools to relieve your spirit's discomfort and conquer the attached "body thetans". In a process akin to a pyramid scheme, there are levels to your "thetanship." The ultimate goal is to become an "Operating Thetan."

Because of the nature of its core beliefs, Scientology has undergone a lot of scrutinies. They are the subject of several accusations, such as being a cult and having a criminal leader. In 1979, Ron Hubbard had been convicted of fraud in France, where he was sentenced four years in prison. In my research, I found the following quote and could not resist including it because I cannot make this stuff up. In a 2008 CNN interview, church spokesman Tommy Davis was asked whether the basic tenet of the Church of Scientology was to rid the body of space alien parasites." I'm sure they did not mean to come across as condescending and obtuse, but it almost seems to be a fair, albeit simplistic, summary of Scientology's principles.

Voodoo

As with many alternative religions with roots in traditional theology, Voodoo is essentially a combination of Catholicism and African beliefs. The intermingling of these two faiths occurred when the slaves who were captured from Africa and sold into slavery began to merge their native ideas with their captor's views. The slave's customary African traditions and their practice were strictly forbidden to strip the Africans of their heritage and maintain control over their religious beliefs. The slaves began to equate the God of Christianity and Catholic saints with their African god Bandye, or Damballah in the Caribbean, and other African ancestral gods. This merge of gods and religious practices served to create what we now refer to as the Voodoo way of life. Some Vodouisants might explicitly identify themselves as Christian or Catholic if asked their religious affiliation even though they practice Vodou as a way of life.

The West African roots of Voodoo come from the ancient practices of ancestor worship and animism, which is the belief that spirits inhabit all things, including animals and plants. They believe that Bondye and all of the familial spirits of old are available to us for guidance and influence within the physical plane. They reside in a realm that is invisible to the naked eye, yet is as intertwined with our reality as though they were still alive. Although Bondye is the highest God or creator, Bondye is not a god to whom we beseech with prayer our requests for assistance in earthly matters. Voodoo practitioners can seek daily aid from the many spirits of the ancestors called Lwa and from mother nature to help with their problems such as love, money, or business.

Because of the representations that you may have seen in movies, you stereotypically think of scary dolls, beheaded chickens, and hexes when Voodoo's subject comes to mind. This thought process is not far from the actual mark in theory but serves to present an oversimplified description of this very colorful religion. Voodoo does incorporate the utilization of voodoo dolls and animal sacrifice into its core rituals. Depending on the request, the animal sacrifices are necessary to provide spiritual nourishment for the Lwa in gratitude for their intervention on the practitioner's behalf. The participants of the ritual then consume the physical remains.

The practices of sticking needles into voodoo dolls to manipulate other humans are mostly urban legend. However, they do dedicate dolls to certain Lwa depending on the influence they are requesting. Another practice is the use of veve, which are symbols that they draw into flour, cornmeal, or other powdery substances as a form of fortune-telling or spiritual communication of answers to the believers' questions. These symbols are earmarked for specifics types of requests and are assigned to the corresponding Lwa associated with each application.

Because of their roots in Christian Catholicism, practitioners of Voodoo do also believe in the afterlife. It is their belief that good souls go to a version of heaven while evil souls are banished to roam the Earth as bodiless spirits.

Witchcraft

I hope you have found these shards of a view into these alternative religions fascinating thus far; I know I have. I have saved the subject of witchcraft last because it covers a massive amount of variations and information. As a member of the Universal Life Church organization, I received an email that stated that the witches are banding together to hex the police and protect the protesters during this time of Black Lives Matter in response to police brutality and murder of Black men. For some reason, this show of solidarity and support from a practicing witches group is a pleasant surprise. I might never have considered that witches would care to participate in social and political affairs in this manner. I find it refreshing that they have joined in such a politically explosive activist movement. Their involvement caused me to pause and reflect upon the preconceived notions and limited view that I fostered about witches in general. I welcome you to do the same.

I will do my due diligence to condense this thesis in a respectful manner that is both comprehensive and appropriate without losing too much detail that symbolizes this castigation. To that end, I will focus on modern witchcraft as this subject has a history that spans 1000's of years in many different forms and iterations. The most significant organized representation of witchcraft in this age identify as Wiccans.

Wicca

I hear that there is a saying that says if you ask ten Wiccans what their spiritual beliefs are, you will get 15 different answers. I do not personally know this to be accurate. Still, the idea sounds plausible because Wicca does not have a holy book or a designated governing body like most religions. But if you were to credit any one particular person as the originator of modern-day Wicca, you would name Gerald Gardner. In the late 1950's, he organized a secret society of people who pledged an oath and endured an initiation process to join the witches' community.

As popularity spread, the original group's offshoots began to form and evolve the content, rituals, and beliefs of the group.

We will look at some of the overarching global beliefs that are the result of their evolution. Wiccans believe in their gods' polarity as both male and female deities such as Isis and Osiris or Apollo and Athena. No matter which group you decide to join, there is most likely an initiation process that symbolizes your rebirth that you will have to go through to gain membership into the coven. There are degrees of advancement that you can achieve that will elevate you to the level of High Priest or Priestess.

Wiccans practice the arts of magic and spell work across the board because, for them, magic is a natural part of engaging with the natural world. Their spells and magic incorporate earth elements such as crystals, herbs, wands, and candles. They also believe in the afterlife; it is not uncommon for them to participate in seances to make contact with the spirit realm. Tarot, runes, and astrology are standard tools used in witchcraft, but these practices go back millennia and are not new concepts specific to this group.

Their beliefs include belief in the divinity of nature, karma and the afterlife, ancestry, holidays, personal responsibility, causing no harm, and respect for opposing viewpoints. We will look at a few of these beliefs relevant to the purposes of this book and the addiction of religion that translate into the Wiccan world as well. First, there is the belief in karma and the afterlife, which suggests that what you do in this life will impact you either positively or negatively in the next life. You can look at it as a cosmic payback system in a sense. They call it the three-fold return, which means that anything you do to another human being will revisit you three-fold. Additionally, the belief in the afterlife negates the belief in the concept of sin or the existence of heaven or hell.

Secondly, the notion of personal responsibility advocates individual accountability for any actions that you might take during your daily life. This responsibility suggests that with the action taken, you are thereby willing and agreeing to accept all consequences that arise as a result of your actions. And finally, I find the idea of respect for other's beliefs interesting. However, they do practice proselytizing new followers. But they feel like you should make up your mind about what spiritual path works best for you.

To conclude, it is important to note certain critical elements of alternative religious dogmata. First, and I feel one of the more poignant features is the derivation or inclusion of Christian theology. Satanism seems to desecrate and to posit ideas that are polar opposite to Christian views. Second, even in the case of Scientology, there is still an entity that presents as more significant than yourself in these religions in the form of Satan, gods, or otherworldly beings.

Next Steps and Takeaways from this chapter:

The Debate: Can you be a true Christian and seek advice from practitioners of witchcraft or Voodoo to get help?

It is difficult for most to imagine how an individual can abandon all concepts of humanity and goodwill towards your fellow man to become immersed in a dark world that spits in the face of the basic understanding of morality. It may be equally challenging to imagine the possibility of alien lifeforms impacting our earthly lives. And should we be concerned about witches casting spells that could potentially bring harm to us or our loved ones? But could the reality be that those who follow these darker paths are at the same time exploring the darker possibilities of God?

At the very least, you now know much more about these alternative religions than you knew before. And before you race towards judgment and dismissal of these ideas, I challenge you first to imagine how bizarre, ridiculous, or far-fetched your own beliefs might look to members of one of these communities or someone else who believes differently than you do. I would encourage you to engage in an active conversation with someone that you might encounter who participates in either an opposing religious philosophy or one of the practices mentioned above in this chapter. Don't be afraid to hear a different point of view or even to make a new friend.

***Meet Byron is his own words*:**

My relationship with religion seems a little different than others to me. I was raised by a single mother who did her best to get us to church as often as possible, considering where we lived. My mom wanted us to go to a Baptist Church, but we stayed in a very Catholic area outside of Atlanta. In other words, my mom wanted us to go to a black church, but we stayed around nothing but white churches. So, our only option was to get up early take us to a church off in Atlanta. She finally found New Birth Baptist Church back in the early 90s with Bishop Eddie Long.

We'd always go to the early morning service at 7 AM, and we stayed close to an hour away, so that meant I had to get up extra early, which I never liked. Nevertheless, we did it on occasion. I know that we did go enough to where Bishop Eddie long was the one who baptized me (which kind of concerns me, but oh well). I'm not going to get into the history, but if you don't know who Bishop Eddie long is, just Google him. Nothing happened at all like it does in the Catholic church, but it sometimes makes you pause and think that you have to watch a lot of people in power and entrusted. We probably stopped attending a little bit after the church moved and became a megachurch in my church experience began to fade too. If there was one thing that I did get from the church, nobody knew the truth and that everything should be questioned.

As I got older, I began to do my research on what this universe is all about and how we got here. One thing that I did derive from all that is that something happened worldwide a thousand years ago that everybody had to write texts about what was going on. There was some sort of awakening for the people of the ancient world, and I genuinely believe they did not know what was going on. I think all the people around the world wrote about what they saw in a metaphoric Style, and these writings is where the start of religion was derived from. Now I like to think outside the box a lot, and what I truly think people were seeing was beings from outside our planet. And these beings are so advanced with intelligence that they seem to like gods descending from the heavens to the ancient world. Now I like to think outside the box, and for some people, this aspect might be hard to swallow, but to me, it makes perfect sense.

I try to back up my ideological thinking with science. And IF the science is correct, then the universe is way too vast and way too old for humankind to be the only civilization out there. So, let's break down the science real quick. It's said that the universe is 13.9 billion years old and about 13.9 billion light-years across. A light-year is how far a beam of light can travel in one year. Light travels at 186,000 miles per second, and at that speed, after 1 year, that beam of light will have traveled right under 6 trillion miles. Now multiply that by 13.9 billion, and you have the size (SUPPOSEDLY) all of the observable universe. These numbers are mind-numbing and unfathomable.

The closest way I can perceive it in my head is if you were to take all the world's oceans and put them together, and then take one grain of sand and throw it into the ocean, then that grain of sand would probably be the size of the Earth, and all the world's oceans would be the universe. To me, to think that we are the only intelligent life out there is pretty laughable. And if life has had more time to mature on other worlds, then their intelligence could be far greater than ours, and what they could achieve could probably seem like magic to us, or god-like. In a nutshell, I firmly believe that all biblical texts referred to off-world entities that intervened on our behalf to better humankind.

Think to yourself for a second, could the Egyptians build the Great Pyramids as big as they are by themselves? Engineers say that even today, with the technology that we have, it is damn near impossible to construct something like that. Also, many hieroglyphics on walls and in tombs in Egypt depict different types of ships and crafts that look like they can fly. And finally, the Great Pyramids are located in the direct geographical center of Earth. And the pyramids line up perfectly with the arrangement of Orion's Belt in the night sky. Maybe it's all just a coincidence, but I don't think so.

I believe there was some divine intervention that helped them become one of the best-known ancient civilizations ever. If you do enough research, you can find evidence of "divine intervention" in every aspect of the past. Just look at how our society in the US has progressed in the past 100 years. A hundred years ago, everything was pretty much running by steam or something of that nature. Fast forward to 1947 when a supposed UFO crashed in Roswell, New Mexico. Now all of a sudden, technology booms. We find out how to make an atomic bomb; we travel to space, make computers and TVs, and progress to where we're now with pretty much handheld computers in the palm of our hand that can pretty much do anything or get any type of information that we need.

I don't think it's a coincidence. I believe these beings have been here since we've been here and have helped us progress as a species. We might have come from them, who really knows? I firmly believe that the stories about the gods from heaven and how religion started comes from these entities. Do your own research and be the judge for yourself. Don't let others try to brainwash you into thinking what they believe.

With all that being said, the universe all this in it, and all that's beyond it, I had to come from some type of higher power. What that power is, I have no idea. I don't think that our human brains can perceive what it is, so we try to make the best of what we can perceive and come up with our religions and reason for being here. If my last statements didn't kind of blow your mind, this one might take you over the top. I believe what we all perceive as reality may be some kind of super elaborate computer simulation, like the movie The Matrix. Scientists say that down to the smallest fundamental element that our technology allows us to see, everything is pixelated, just like on the computer.

CHAPTER 3 CULTS: WHAT'S THE DRAW

> *"If religion were true, its followers would not try to bludgeon their young into an artificial conformity; but would merely insist on their unbending quest for truth, irrespective of artificial backgrounds or practical consequences." H. P. Lovecraft*

If religion is an addiction, then members of a cult are the heroin addicts of religious culture. I was swinging on a pendulum of indecision as to whether or not cults should have their own chapter or fall under another subject as a sub-topic. The universe would not allow me to delete this chapter. Therefore, I am going to give this subject my sincerest effort. Cults may be the one area of religion where people might postulate that cult followers are the most deluded. For this reason, shining a light upon the nature and characteristics of cult-like behavior and tendencies may be the catalyst that will illuminate the need or the desire to pull someone from the chasm of lostness. I make it a practice not to judge anyone's belief system as I believe they are correct if they serve your soul's purpose. But cult communities tend to be groups that preclude individual choice; therefore, they open themselves to scrutiny from those on the outside looking into their practices.

I searched for a definition of the word cult that I feel best exemplifies the impact of the nature of this type of religious group. The very word cult is a pejorative term in nature. There were two definitions from yourdictionary.com that present a reasonable explanation of what the cult represents. The first definition suggests that a cult is a quasi-religious group, often living in a colony and typically with a charismatic leader who indoctrinates members with beliefs regarded as unorthodox or extremist. The second definition explains that a cult is a group of people with extreme dedication to an individual leader or set of ideas that are often viewed as odd by others, or is an excessive and misplaced admiration for someone or something, or is something prevalent among a particular segment of society.

What I am finding to be two critical indicators of cult communities is the absence of the development and fulfillment of self and the propagation of its leader in a way that may lead to its members' detriment. Ironically, most of the cults that I researched have kernels of origin from traditional religions. To establish the credibility of their beliefs, cult leaders often bastardize portions of the Bible. Their leaders interweave religious ideologies into their philosophies. They tend to take a more literal and extreme approach to some part of a recognized traditional religion and then exploit the ethos in a self-serving manner. It is not uncommon to be a member of conventional religion but have a leader who veers off the established path of the religion's objective to evolve into a cult-like situation.

Snake Handling

An example would be the Pentecostals, who are known for handling deadly snakes and openly drinking poison as a part of their worship rituals. This group has focused on the scripture in Mark 16:17 that reads, 'And these signs shall follow them that believe: in my name, they will cast out demons; they will speak in new tongues; they will pick up serpents, and if they drink any deadly thing, it will not hurt them; they will lay hands on the sick, and they will recover." The rationale is pretty simple. They believe that they can do exactly what this scripture suggests in the literal sense.

For other Christians, this proposition can be viewed as quite bizarre because many of their members are maimed or even killed by these deadly snakes handled by the worshipper as they participate in their religious ceremonies. The congregation simply believed that anyone who is bitten by snakes or harmed by the poison lacks the Holy Spirit's presence and the appropriate amount of faith needed to protect them from harm, as indicated in the scriptures. After a follower is bitten or poisoned, the group will pray for this poor soul. If they should die, death is an indication of God's will being fulfilled. Many will go to the hospital to seek treatment for their injuries. They are forgiven or not forgiven by the church, depending on social expectations.

The mismatch is that the inclusion of these scriptures into the biblical text is controversial amongst theologians. Some suggest that these last scriptures were not included in the original text. Which raises the question, aren't ALL of these scriptures written by men anyway? Yet again, we have to take it on blind faith that the translators employed by King James got the translations of the second-hand accounts of other men of what Jesus is supposed to have said is correct. See the fly in the ointment here?

When I read these scriptures, I interpreted them to mean that if I happened to come across a snake or deadly poison, I am under God's protection. I do not recall a single instance in the Bible that might suggest that anyone intentionally included poison and snakes as a practice of their faith. Thousands of years before Christ, Moses threw down his rod, and it turned into a serpent, but he was instructed by God personally to do so. The Apostle Paul got accidentally bitten by a snake, but he didn't go out of his way to intentionally handle the snake. Also, in I Corinthians 10:9 NIV (also written by Paul, who got bitten, but written as a quote from Jesus), reads, "We should not test Christ, as some of them did--and were killed by snakes."

It would be insane to intentionally pick up a lethal viper and roll the dice with my life to prove a sacred point. But to these devout worshippers, they do not view their acts as tempting God but rather fulfilling the scriptures in the act of obedience. But this raises the question, what would God get out of His people gambling their lives with poisonous snakes? And what point would God be making by demanding such risky demonstrations of loyalty from his people? In cult environments, it is ubiquitous to act on beliefs that others view as detrimental to the follower. Remember, the Manson girls shaved their heads and carved an X in their foreheads in the exhibition of their dedication to their leader.

By nature, cults tend to be pits of isolation, feigned hope, and promised security. The cult environment creates a perfect Petri dish to breed the impression of belonging and salvation. Anything or anyone that usurps an individual's opportunity to think freely, leave voluntarily, or develop spiritually is exhibiting the attributes of a predator, a person, or an animal that hunts a smaller, weaker person or animal. And in my mind, it is this predatory tendency that reveals the extremist nature of the cult environment and simultaneously posits the notion that a cult operates outside of the parameters of organized religion. People are willing to succumb to the demands of the cult environment because it cultivates an intimacy between its leader and its followers that brandishes a devotion akin to romantic love.

Unlike most organized religions, the cult family's nucleus centers around an earthly leader rather than a specific deity. Compliance, discipline, authority, and unabashed reliance is entrusted to either a God-like figure (in the case of David Koresh) or a self-proclaimed God-like representative (in the case of Jim Jones) that is the leader of the group.

Jim Jones

For example, Jim Jones initially presented as a charismatic evangelical man of God who preached social and racial equality, both of which are noteworthy principles and evidence of a somewhat noble beginning. However, as time went on, like most cult leaders, his teachings leaned less towards things of God and more toward complete and utter submission to the will and edicts of Jim Jones himself. Had Jones' followers been less devoted to the man, they might have recognized the insanity seeds that were blossoming within Jones. The followers either did not notice or at least acknowledge that Jones was slowly sliding into the abyss of madness, drug abuse, and paranoia. He proclaimed himself God—Judge, jury, and executioner —over his flock.

In the end, he would require his supporters to offer their very lives in allegiance to him as a leader and to his cause. The requirement of devotion to its leader is a crucial indicator that you may be in a cult situation and not a religious organization. Although throughout history, "holy men" have presented as representatives of God, such as the likes of Jesus, Buddha, or Muhammad. In a cult environment, the leader introduces himself as equal to God. The devoted followers place the desires and commands of this leader above their own in complete surrender to avoid dire consequences either in this life or promise of negative reprisals in the next.

Tricks of the Trade

Aside from the deification of its leader, another standard tool in the cult arsenal is isolation from friends, family, and anyone who might influence the believer to question the guidance provided by the cult leader. Cult leaders often leverage covert brainwashing tactics to influence the followers, such as long periods of teaching during extended bouts of sleep deprivation. The introduction of psychedelic drugs is often incorporated into the program. Control over sexual activities such as forced abstinence or sexual relations being controlled by the leader's approval or limited to sex with the leader. The aim is to convince you that what they are teaching you is for your good and that if you want—(place what they promise you here)—salvation, healing, happiness, enlightenment, etc., you must comply with their demands to obtain it.

Peer-pressure is a decisive instrument in the cult cache that serves to reinforce the mind control tactics. Recruits are not given much time for contemplation but are pressured to join and accept the group's beliefs. This ploy preys upon an individual's sense of self-worth and desire to belong and fit into the group. You are strongly encouraged to listen and learn while being urged not to question or defy the cult's ideas. Your peers are also deeply involved with your assimilation into the group. They may watch your every move and report back to the leader examples of any suspicious behavior they might observe. In this way, you are not allowed any expression of autonomy and self-reflection. You must conform to the cult's rules, and your new friends are there to make sure that you do just that!

Most churches have "alter calls" (an invitation to accept Jesus into your heart) at the end of the service, during which they kindly open the doors of the church, allowing visitors to join the fellowship. But rarely, if ever, will they follow you home and continue the pitch to get you to join. And if they do this, I would recommend that you run. However, cults are in it to play the long game, and everybody knows the rules but you. They will wear down your resistance, your questions, and your will to confront them until you simply give in and accept their requirements. They will have opinions about every facet of your life. For example, they may scrutinize how you dress, what you eat, and how you raise your children. There is nothing sacred or off-limits.

While isolation from outside influences is essential, segregation and mistrust within the organization are equally useful. The "tattle tale" system of accountability fosters a sense of suspicion of fellow members. Each seeks to ingratiate themselves closer and closer to the leader by demonstrating unrelenting devotion and implicit loyalty. In this way, the followers are only allowed to truly trust the leader, which further feeds into the leader's narcissistic sense of invulnerability. Many cult leaders brandish fear of an impending event that will bring about the end of the world. Followers still believe even though the world has failed to end by their predictions because, by that point, they are so far gone and invested in the cult that it is challenging to face the fact that they were wrong.

Cults tend to exhibit anti-social, self-destructive, and oppressive behaviors, which ultimately lead to their demise as an entity. Both Waco and Jonestown experienced fatal ends due to the inability of their leaders to function socially within the world. For this reason, rarely do cults survive over several generations, like most established religions. Charles Manson's cult group, though willing to murder at his behest, did not create a belief system that was strong enough to reach over generations or reach people who were not counterculture, naïve and impressionable gullible. Manson has many fans, but there are not nearly enough followers to suggest that his ideology is true religion.

Koresh

In Waco, Texas, the original group of Davidians was founded in 1934 by Victor Houteff. The Davidians are an offshoot of the Seventh Day Adventist Church, who rejected Victor as a heretic for his conflicting beliefs. But the world did not become aware of this group until many years later when David Koresh would succeed Lois Roden as their prophet. Koresh had an affair with the seventy-odd-year-old woman and purportedly got her pregnant. She reportedly miscarried the baby. For the group, the older woman's impregnation would be proof positive that God touched Koresh. This revelation catapulted him into the position from which he would oust Lois and assume the leadership role for the group now called The Branch Davidians.

The followers of David Koresh are so enamored with him and his teachings, many of the survivors still believe in his impending return. They believe in his authority even though his actions led to the death of their family members and loved ones.

Leaders like Koresh build credibility by claiming to have exclusive access to or an understanding of God's will beyond that which is available to the common everyday man. Koresh would ban all sexual activity, even between man and wife, save sexual relations with himself. He would father 17 children with various members of the sect. Koresh also incorporated rock and roll music into his services, which greatly appealed to the young members who would join the group.

It is easy for some to fall for this type of rhetoric because they are already searching for answers. Suppose someone can speak with conviction that they have found those answers. They can deliver the message in a passionate way that somehow resonates with an inkling of what the searcher already believes to be accurate. In that case, the searcher will trust them, follow them, and even worship them.

The Children of God

The Children of God cult was founded in 1968 by David Brandt Berg, another deviation from Christianity. Like many cult leaders, Berg was formerly a pastor and evangelist in the Christian community. He broke away from the church to prey upon the lost souls of the hippie movement and other outcasts of society to form the Light Club, which later became known as the Children of God. Berg also changed his name to Moses David. In addition to the name, he borrowed polygamy from the old testament philosophies. He proclaimed himself to be the "End Time" prophet and a key leader in the imminent second coming of Christ. He demanded that his followers quit all employment to become full-time missionaries for his ministry. Later on, he deployed to the women a practice he called "flirty fishing," an idea loosely based on Jesus' petition to his disciples to be fishers of men. To woo potential followers, the women would frequent bars and seduce male customers with sex and whatever sexual persuasion needed to get the men to join the group.

It is from this point that the cult takes a more sexually-oriented turn. Its followers were encouraged to give up all earthly possessions and contact with the outside world. Sex with children is not only permissible but strongly encouraged. They purport that children can understand and participate fully in sexual acts from a very young age. Moses David found it fitting to indulge in sexual proclivities with as many of these children as he deems fulfilling to his needs. In many cults, the self-important leader has considered himself the authority of mandating how sexual behavior should or should not be permitted within the group and with whom. Pedophilia appears to be a recurring theme in many cults. When the leader finds a way to twist the Bible or other holy books to claim that child sex is permissible, there can be a particular appeal to those who have such pedophilic appetites. The Mormons have been accused of similar beliefs and practices as they relate to children.

Other Cults of Recent Times

There are countless cult groups that I could mention here. But then you could write an entire book on this subject, and many have already done so. But I will call out a few more before we move on. The Heaven's Gate cult was unique because they believed in UFO's. It is poignant to mention this group because, as I mentioned earlier, sometimes belief in one attribute of a cult can blind you to many of the oddities that the cult promotes. This group consisted of mostly scientific and computer savvy, highly intelligent people. It's founder Marshal Applewhite, preyed upon the shared belief in UFOs to reproduce his ideas of an afterlife with the aliens aboard an extraterrestrial spaceship. His teachings so brainwashed his members that the women cut their hair to hide their femininity, and many of the men castrated each other. They wanted to become asexual beings. You may smirk and chuckle at these ideas while envisioning weirdos with aluminum foil on their heads. Still, this group was so devoted to these beliefs in extraterrestrial studies that they went on to commit the largest mass suicide on American soil to date.

NXIVM is yet another cult group that was fashioned more along the lines of a pyramid scheme turned cult. Its leader Keith Raniere evolved his alleged "self-help" group into an international sex cult. The chosen women were branded with his symbol on their hips with a branding iron, forcing them to be his sex slaves. They accuse him of being a charlatan that stole thousands of dollars from people to take these self-improvement classes. Over 80 members later sued him with a 200-page lawsuit detailing his crimes of fraud. This example goes to show that you can find yourself caught up in a cult or scam with the most innocent of intentions. You must stay alert and note any behaviors that we have identified in this book that might be clues to a potentially dangerous situation.

From Cult to Religion

A cult would need to evolve a system of teachers to carry on its message, which would require a hierarchy of leadership that would share the news beyond the fold of a small group. In most cases, the inherent narcissism of the leader disallows their ability to share power and the scope of the delegation that would allow them to grow sustainably. The capacity to segment such influence, (albeit in a very selective and controlled way), has enabled the Church of Mormon or Church of the Latter-Day Saints religion to evolve beyond cult status. They have grown into a culture that has thrived over 100 years and has followers worldwide due to their missionary efforts.

Founded by Joseph Smith circa the 1820s, he claimed that at the behest of an angel, he went on to find a buried book written on golden plates. These plates were said to contain the ancient religious history of the people in America. Joseph translated these golden plates to create the Book of Mormon. This group blended the beliefs of Christianity with their brand of religious history that insists that Adam and Eve lived in Missouri. The holy trinity is three separate Gods, and there are three levels of heaven. And because of their missionary efforts, there are more Mormons around the world than in America. However, this religion has endured much scrutiny for their beliefs that society might deem immoral, such as child marriage and the factions that practice God-ordained polygamy.

Ironically, Christianity was considered to be a cult at its inception. And many of what we call religious denominations were named factions at some point. Part of the allure of being attracted to a cult community may begin with the seed of some core belief that the potential follower may have but may be considered strange or taboo by others. Focus on this one particular value may allow the devotee to ignore parts of the cult that may otherwise be seen as inappropriate by others. The most important thing to know is that it is never too late to leave an unsafe situation. The mistake or poor judgment that led you towards a cult can be corrected by making a conscious decision to save yourself.

Next Steps and Takeaways from this chapter:

The Debate: Do loved ones have the right to try to force someone to leave their cult?

The next steps for this chapter are to contemplate a series of questions. Examine the leadership of the religious organization that you are currently associating with today. Is your leader the primary focus of the ministry or religious group? Are your individual needs being met? Or is the emphasis always on the needs of the minister? Or is the focus on the furtherment of the cult or group itself? Are you free to express your thoughts and to share your point of view? Are excessive demands upon your time and unrealistic financial obligations the primary motivation of your leadership?

Are you required to give all of your money and possessions to the group? Are there sexual demands or restrictions placed upon you and the other members? Does your organization tangibly contribute to the wellbeing of the community? Is your group exclusive and isolated? Is your leader placed on a pedestal, or is he or she approachable by anyone? These are the manner of questions that you have to ask yourself to ensure that you are not sucked into something that might be very disappointing and detrimental to your personal growth and development. You owe it to yourself to get out if you are not healthily celebrating your freedom and spirituality. You know the answers to these questions deep down inside. If you find yourself rationalizing, making excuses, or creating justifications for strange behaviors or rules in your group, trust your soul's instinctual guidance.

Meet Ashleigh in her own words:

Often being a member of The Church of Jesus Christ of latter-day saints, I'm asked these questions, i.e., "Do you believe in Jesus Christ?" Yes! He is the chief cornerstone of the church that bears His name-The Church of Jesus Christ of Latter-day Saints. "Do you believe in the bible?" Yes! The Bible is the word of God. It leads us to Jesus Christ and shows us how to follow His perfect example. I would like to bear my testimony that I know this church is true and that gossip is true. I'm an imperfect person, and I sometimes can't put my thoughts and words down in an eloquent manner or even grammatically correct! Nevertheless, I pray that the Holy Spirit can convey my feelings to you as you read this. I hope you can feel the love I have for you and our savior Jesus Christ. I have a testimony of Jesus Christ, and I know that he lives. He is the son of God and my redeemer. He died on the cross on and paid for my sins. He knows me and loves me. He knows each and every one of us and loves us.

I have a testimony of the atonement of Jesus Christ and that I have received it. His atonement helped heal me in my recovery from sins and affections. The power of the atonement is real. I have felt his grace. I am forever grateful to Him. I believe in the Bible and the Book of Mormon, and that they are holy scriptures to help guide us back to our beloved Heavenly parents.

I know that there is a God who is our Heavenly Father and a God who Is our Heavenly Mother, and we lived in the pre-mortal existence before coming to earth, and we are their children. I believe in the prophets' testimonies. I know we have a living Prophet today who is President Russell M. Nelson, and I sustain him and know he speaks the truth. My spirit is overflowing with love and warmth as I type these words down, and I hope you can feel them. ❤

I say these things in the name Jesus Christ,

Amen

CHAPTER 4 RACISM AND RELIGION

> *"We were all human until race disconnected us, religion separated us, politics divided us, and wealth classified us." Unknown*

Religion can be a fundamental part of your identity as a person. "I am a Christian" or "I am a Buddhist." The word religion comes from a Latin word that means "to tie or bind together." Modern dictionaries define religion as "an organized system of beliefs and rituals centering on a supernatural being or beings." To belong to a religion often means more than sharing its beliefs and participating in its rituals; it also means being part of a community and, sometimes, a culture. But what if your religious culture perpetuates hatred against other human beings at its core? What if your religion teaches you that you are superior and intrinsically more intelligent than other members of the human race by virtue of the color of your skin? How does one navigate a world where devotion to your God means the violation of another person and their God?

I read many definitions of the word racism. Still, I like the following description: the belief that different races possess distinct characteristics, abilities, or qualities, uniquely to distinguish them as inferior or superior to one another. Most people would have to admit that they have demonstrated prejudice against another person or race for one reason or another. But there is a distinct difference between prejudice and bigotry.

Racial bias typically derives from a place of ignorance. Prejudice is having a preconceived opinion of another person based upon stereotypes or other people's views that are not from personal experience. An example of discrimination and stereotyping against black people would be the notion that all black people like chicken and watermelon. The truth is that almost everyone loves chicken and watermelon no matter their race. And my husband, who is a black man, does not like watermelon at all. How funny is that? What about the notion that white people can't play basketball as well as black people? Or all Chinese people can't drive? I could be ridiculously offensive and note a million stupid stereotypes that many people believe to be true simply because they are too lazy to get to know other races.

The words racism and religion look to be diametrically opposing words that should not be put together within the same phrase as companions but rather as antagonists. However, protagonists of racism have historically endorsed their hatred as a God-given right. In my mind, the paradigm of "God" supported racism is the ultimate contradiction and the epitome of irrational behavior. Many racist factions hold fast to strong beliefs that they have intertwined with religious ideologies at its core. Some religions proliferate racism as an imagined direction from God himself.

In Judaism and Christianity, the Bible encourages the racial separatism of God's people from both other races and the people of "the world," respectively. Human beings are known to form groups of those with similar interests. How else can you reconcile belief in scripture that reads "Love they neighbor" but then mistreat a neighbor of a different race?

Early America

In what can only be viewed as irony, America has a regrettable history steeped in religious elitism and racism. Paradoxically, the first Puritan settlers left England to escape religious persecution only to launch their own religious persecution in the newly established colonies. They desired to create the pure Christian church, which would denounce Catholicism and all other religions entirely. The indigenous Indians that occupied the new world never stood a chance against the God of the white man. They thought Indians to be savage, ungodly, and heathens because they did not know nor wish to know the "true god" of the puritans.

The Native Americans had their own religious beliefs and practices, which were entirely disregarded by the marauding and pillaging new colonists. They thought the Natives were less than secondhand citizens in their own country, which was systematically and deplorably stripped away from them by our founding fathers. Europeans have a vast history of invading lands all around the world and annihilating the beliefs of those indigenous people of the nations they have stolen—all in the name of their God.

These same founding fathers went on to enslave Africans, exploit Chinese immigrants, and nearly annihilate the indigenous Indian tribes here in America. They had the unmitigated gall to force all of these people to embrace their religious faith that did not include them in God's embrace and favor as equal participants.

White Supremacist

Although several offshoots are atheists, many white supremacists here in America claim to have a Christian identity despite their horrific racist ideologies. Among their beliefs are anti-Semitic conspiracy theories, separatism of the white race from all races that are non-white, and violence to further their cause. They live by their interpretation of the Bible because their heinous, cruel, and despicable violence against African Americans and other minorities and open displays of hostility and hatred do not support Christ's teachings. Furthermore, Jesus Christ is of Jewish descent, which is in direct conflict with their anti-Semitic beliefs. They have manipulated the history of Jesus' birth and nationality in a conspicuously compelling way that claims that Jesus is a white man to support their political agenda. They have had to reconstruct history to validate and establish this fact to not diverge with their anti-Semitic point of view.

The Christian Identity Church is one of today's religious hate groups. Its pastor Thomas Robb is a long-time leader of the Ku Klux Klan. Not only is this group racist against all non-whites, but they are also against the LGBTQ community. Kingdom Identity Ministries is another Christian identifying church hate group replete with bible courses, seminars, and training books. James Wickstrom, who claims to be a minister, disseminates pomposity that calls for the complete extermination of the Jews on his radio show and in his sermons. America's Promise ministries have a more literal approach to interpreting the Bible. They have decided that Jesus was white and is the champion of the cause of the white man. There are members of this group who have ostensibly committed murder, acts of terrorism, abortion clinic bombings, and robbery. This kind of violent behavior is not very Christ-like. Would you agree?

Additionally, I made a point to mention covert white supremacists here in this chapter. Still, there is a gamut of white Americans who are members of traditional religious organizations such as Southern Baptist, for example, who are equally prejudiced and racist1 in their beliefs. It feels like an oxymoron to say that someone is a racist Christian and proud of it.

Moreover, I feel like I have to admit that the illustration of racist Christians is most disparaging to me because of all of the religious leaders, Jesus implicitly spread a message of love and tolerance. I comprehend neither the need nor the logic for identifying with religion if you have to pervert its teachings. In my mind, this is a clear example of the state of denial and evidence of an active case of the addiction of religion if I have ever seen one. Although as strange as it may sound, these people are still a part of me, so I cannot hate them. They represent the ugly side of God. Don't believe me? What if I were to tell you that God says He is both good and evil even in the Bible, would you believe me then? In Isaiah 45:7 God says this,

> *"I form the light, and create darkness: I make peace, and create evil: I the Lord do all these things."*

We will just let that marinate. And for you theologians, here is my homework. The Hebrew word for evil is רַע, rah, which occurs 664 times in the Old Testament and translates as evil, wickedness, disaster, harm, bad, fierce, downcast, ugly, etc. Yessir, God is all of those things. So, whether we like it or not, could it be that God is racist? We will discuss this idea later on in our text when we address morality. There is no right and wrong because it is all the same thing—it is all relative. Nation of Islam Racism is an equal opportunity beast and not exclusive to a white supremacist.

The Nation of Islam

Racism is an equal opportunity beast and not exclusive to a white supremacist. The Nation of Islam vehemently denies the allegations. However, like white supremacists, the Nation of Islam is cited as having a rich history of anti-Semitism. The great Minister Louis Farrakhan is quoted as calling those of Jewish descent "devils," Satanic, and termites. I watched a video in which his disdain for the Jews was quite prolific and unabashed. They also claim that this organization blames Jews for having a significant role in the slave trade from Africa, attempting to control the economy, and sucking the American people's blood.

Next Steps and Takeaways from this Chapter:

The debate: Can a person be both racist and a good person simultaneously?

This chapter reveals a less philanthropical stance that religion can take when taught by people who have their own personal agendas. This begs the question: Can anyone make up their own rules and call it religion as long they throw their version of God as the originator of those beliefs and as justification for those same beliefs? If so, do we have a responsibility to identify the agenda, judge those beliefs, and challenge the origin of said beliefs?

And is it fair to project your prejudices and racist views upon your children? And what of the manipulation of youth who might be vulnerable to racist opinions based on poor familial backgrounds or low self-esteem? How many people learn to follow racial profiling and prejudice when incarcerated and need to join a group for survival?

I challenge you to examine yourself and honestly assess if and why you may have prejudices against any particular race and isolate where those views derived. Did you learn it from your parents, friends, or someone you look up to for approval? Know that even if you love someone racist, this does not mean that you have to accept their views as your own to appreciate them as a person. If they will desert you if you do not share their beliefs, then I would recommend that you try to understand why this person is so important to you. What are you missing that you have to compromise your soul to have this person's approval? That is your work.

Meet The Homeless Alcoholic in his own words:

Religion is powerful. You got to have faith. Religion is very, very, very. Religion is powerful. I came, I-I came..I was baptized. I-I-I-I was born in "68. I came in the church. And I pray every day. And you got 5 P's: Proper Preparation Prevents Poor Performance. That's five. But you gotta have the power of prayer. You gotta thank God.

When I wake up I say I thank God. I don't say God help me. I say God I thank you for seeing another...I say God I thank you for blessing my DNA. I thank you for Jacob, Isaac, and Abraham. I thank God, when you wake up that's a blessin' That's a blessin'. That's why I got these tatts...that's love. I got faith. I got faith. But faith without works is dead. Amen? Amen. Amen.

PART TWO: HOW WE GOT ADDICTED

CHAPTER 5
BRAINWASHING

> *"True religion, like our founding principles, requires that the rights of the disbeliever be equally acknowledged with those of the believer." A. Powell Davies*

Were you taught to believe in Santa Claus? For most children, Santa is one of the earliest outright lies that parents expose them to with unabashed vigor. "He knows when you've been sleeping. He knows when you're awake. He knows when you've been bad or good, so be good for goodness sake!" The cacophony of little white lies is buried within our psyches and tends to mold how we learn to assimilate with others and feel about ourselves. I have to be good so that Santa will bring the bike I want for Christmas. The reason the lies are so effective upon little children is because of their brain development. Children cannot differentiate between what is real and untrue and readily believe whatever their caregivers teach them. When you layer in the introduction of religion into a child's early development, the brainwashing continues. Whatever sacred creed the child learns is deeply woven into the child's core belief system.

According to the Cambridge dictionary, brainwashing makes someone believe something by repeatedly telling him or her that it is true and preventing any other information from reaching him or her. Many of our fondest and earliest memories involve getting new clothes for an Easter Sunday or ringing in the new year at a Midnight Mass. From birth, those born into religious families begin the indoctrination journey into a spiritual way of thinking. Parents typically learn their ideology from their parents, and so on. For me, it involved memorizing Easter speeches or the simple prayer "Jesus wept" to bless my food.

I recall having to memorize the books of the Bible and participating in scripture memory contests. My mother had us all to quote several scriptures in unison every morning robotically. These were daily affirmations meant to set the tone for a beautiful day as we journeyed on our way to school. We would quote in a humdrum rhythm:

Mom, "What can we do?"

Us, "I can do all things through Christ, which strengthens me."

Mom, "What will God supply?"

Us, "My God will supply all my needs according to His riches and glory by Christ Jesus."

And so forth, I think you get the picture. You may not have had these experiences, but who wasn't taught to say "God bless you" when you hear someone sneeze? Even if you don't like a person, it almost feels blasphemous not to bless them.

The practice of going to a church, a mosque, or any other place of religious worship over an extended amount of time leads to the indoctrination of the child. Like a sponge, the child will consume every word that you teach him about God and the world around her. When those years of teaching continue over a lifetime, it is almost impossible to ultimately convince an individual to believe anything different or be open to a different point of view. This deliberate and continual programming to a particular set of beliefs is, by definition, brainwashing. 80% of the families in America are faithful to their religion of choice. It was not until I reached college to study the history of religion that I had the opportunity to explore beliefs that were different from my own.

Your church might teach you to believe that your religion is correct, but you also learn to discredit others' beliefs. Catholics do not agree with the Jewish faith. Baptists do not agree with the Seventh Day Adventists. Scientologists are known to shun those who step outside of the confines of their beliefs. Each religious circle is sure that their religion is the right way, and the only way to salvation. This is evident when driving in any city in America, and there is a church on nearly every corner. Some churches are across the street from each other, each claiming knowledge of the truth that the others cannot. It is this misapprehension that makes religion both intolerant and fallible. As a result of my travels and studies, I have come to embrace ideas in all religions that serve my sense of highest self while holding none as more significant than the other. I am governed by none save myself.

Throughout history, many humans have declared to have a divine relationship with "God." There are many examples, such as Jesus, Lao Tzu, Muhammad, and countless others, both documented and undocumented. Likewise, you will find their experiences within holy books to share that experience with others in a meaningful way, which led to works such as the Bible, the Koran, the Tao de Ching, and others. Many of us are too lazy to seek the experience of knowing God on our own. It is much easier to accept the findings of another as truth.

We adopt these ideas, and since they sound good, we are all too eager to believe. So, we go with it. You are to accept these beliefs at face value. There is no tangible proof of any of it. Like sheep joyously heading into the slaughter, we yield to the brainwashing with reckless abandon. We need the high, the rush, the rapture of believing. We crave the hope of knowing that something or someone somewhere is running the show. We agree never to have to see it, touch it, or hear it. We only believe. "For the bible tells me so" is our creed.

My husband grew up in a religious family. However, out of 100 Sundays, they may have gone to church 10-15 of those Sundays. Contrarywise, when I grew up, I went to church sometimes seven days per week if there was a revival. However, my husband and I received the same general messages about Jesus, God, and religion that the vast majority of people in the United States receive. Ideas such as treat others the way you want them to treat you, or "Thou shalt not kill" are at face value good suggestions on how to live a moral life. However, absent the religious conditioning that we receive in Sunday school and other sacred forums, how would we define our ethical codes of behavior? Would we hold fast to the same values if we were not trained to believe that we would go to hell? Religion discourages us from making such explorations on our own, and they deem us heretics or worse if we attempt to see things another way.

Thus, many who do not fit into the religious bubble of conformity, are often ostracized and ridiculed. Many develop a break in their sense of moral identity. Those who see or experience religious leaders behave in ways that are incongruent with their teachings foster a similar break in their religious identity. Does the question become how to reconcile the paradox between religion and reality? I learned in the church not to drink alcohol, but I see dad drinking at home. You learn that it is a sin to fornicate or commit adultery at church, but your mom and dad were never married. The pastor's kids are the biggest sinners in the church. Or how about this one, I am kind to others, but they are racist against me. Your brother's black life didn't matter as he was gunned down by racist police. Your parents taught you that black people were less than human and that your race is superior, while Jesus says to love one another.

All of the contradictions can be confusing. And how come it is okay for you, my parents, to be cursing on the way home, having drinks while the game is on, and shacking up while not married, but it's a problem that I identify as being gay? You've been brainwashed into believing you are inherently wrong because you choose a lifestyle that does not fit into the identity that your religion suggests that you should project. How are you supposed to live when you believe you are a sinner because it is all that you have been told for your entire life long? You are literally brainwashed into hating your own self.

The Devil

Humans have become adept at conveniently creating loopholes to explain away aberrant behaviors. One such gap is the invention of "The Devil." We are brainwashed to believe in the existence of Good and Evil. Although the rules say not to do this or, please do that, if you fail to live up to God's expectations, it is not your fault because "the devil made you do it." The rapist and the pedophile are evil because the devil is in them. The wiles of the devil deceive the promiscuous woman and philandering husband. The religious law is absolute, yet the loopholes provide convenient explanations needed to rationalize anomalous behaviors. The Catholics have created their own system that provides a built-in way out of the effects of sin called confession. You can tell this man your sins, and he will forgive your sins by giving you a task to complete. And just like that, your sins are washed away—until next week.

Hypocrisy

No wonder we end up confused. And we have no qualms partying "like it's 1999" on Saturday and then piously attending morning services on Sunday. They have a term for this, and it's called being a hypocrite. A hypocrite is a person who pretends to have virtues, moral or religious beliefs, principles, etc., that he or she does not possess, especially a person whose actions belie stated beliefs. Hypocrisy creates yet another problem for the brainwashed. To obtain the approval of those in the church, you have to present a face that is incongruent with how you live. I have talked to many people who have stopped going to church altogether for this reason. There is a sense of superiority for the outright sinner who embraces his vices and refuses to repent because he is not a "hypocrite." The problem with this point of view is that he is still convinced that the religious edicts are factual and right; I willfully choose not to follow them. Thus, the brainwashing sustains its control over the individual.

Self-Righteousness

No matter what religion you learn, you become spiritually and emotionally tied to those beliefs. The self-righteousness and judgment of others are two of the harmful by-products and cornerstones of your faith. Stones perpetually fly across the sea of glasshouses within which we all abide. We judge her clothes, his hair, his job, their sexuality, their marriage, their children's behavior, her housekeeping, his laziness, their addictions, her promiscuity, his education level, and on, and on, and on, and on, and on. Who went to jail, got pregnant, got fired, is always in charge, and on and on and on. Bones fly out of our mouths that cannot contain the skeletons we have in our own closets.

"I don't understand why judges get paid so much;
others judge me for free." Unknown

Judgment inexplicably perpetuates the brainwashing because if we focus on the flaws in others, we do not have to face our own failures. Religion causes us to strive to hold others to an impossible standard that no one can obtain. It is an ever-loving hamster wheel for the tortured soul. Is there any wonder you are motivated to drink away the pain or swallow the pills that carry you elsewhere on the waves of forgetfulness? You have become addicted to it all.

Control

Some religions have you brainwashed into believing that the church leaders have an indeterminate amount of control over your life. Some leaders control who you will marry, at what age, and to which family. They may go even further into your personal life to give voice to whom you can befriend or associate. Parents rely heavily on guilt trips that are attached to scriptures that command obedience from their children. I have a friend who was forced to marry a man 30 years her senior in obedience to the leaders of her religion. She did so obediently against her wishes. She was taught that marriage was her lot in life, and she accepted it as such. Religion can seek to usurp the authority of your own body by demanding that you refrain from masturbation, birth control, and pre-marital sex.

Arguably, religion is man's attempt to control human behavior. I can remember a time growing up when members of the church were banned from speaking or participating in church services as punishment for minor infractions. They taught us what to wear, how to play, and how to conduct ourselves. God is credited with wanting to control every aspect of our lives, which is in direct contradiction with the misnomer that He has given us free will and free choice.

Financial Brainwashing

Never has religious brainwashing been more self-seeking than when it comes to giving money to the church. You learn that you should provide 10% of your total income to the church every month in most Christian churches. Those who follow Judaism make yearly pledges of money to the church to fulfill their financial obligations. Evangelists proudly laud the fact that God loves a cheerful giver. There is a reason that a lot of pimps later "find God" and become preachers. The same relationship continues under a different umbrella of parasitic behavior. If a preacher gives a good sermon or puts on a good show, the Bible says the "laborer is worth his hire." But you have to know and to understand that the whole performance is just that —a show. And if it makes you feel good, then it's no worse than going to a good movie that made you cry. And, going to a movie might be a lot cheaper than going to some of these churches.

Today some churches request your financial statements when you join the church to give them an idea of how much of a contribution the church can expect to receive from you monthly. There are pastors with entourages, airplanes, and beautiful cars paid for by your tithes and offerings. And like any good pimp, the clothes have to be first class. I am in no way showing disrespect to the hustle. But it is your responsibility to know when you are being hustled. God does not need your money to do anything. Dollars for blessings or miracles is a business that many a televangelist has reaped the benefits of in the form of high living. Fake miracles and promises have gone on for decades since the likes of Jim Jones. Miracle water, prayer cloths, blessed oil, you name it if it costs you money to get it, prepare to be ripped off. You have the faith already within you to receive what you are looking for, so if you get the blessing, it came from you all along.

Next Steps and Takeaways from this Chapter:

The Debate: Should it be illegal for televangelists to charge money for miracles?

After reading this chapter, examine your upbringing. Are the religious beliefs that you now value your own or your parents or some other caregiver? My goal is not to disparage your expectations but to challenge you to look at them. Do you view your religious beliefs a little differently after reading this chapter? Have you been convinced that your ideas are the "ONLY" way to know God? If so, does that statement somehow feel hollower and less convincing in retrospect? Do you see evidence of hypocrisy within your own religious group? Did you use critical thinking and research to derive your current convictions? Can you sit comfortably in the idea that God would only reveal himself to one religion? Can all of the other faiths be wrong?

If you read this chapter and find parallels of brainwashing in your upbringing or even in your life today, your work is to assess your beliefs and discern which ideas are your own or those of other influencers. How do those who share your beliefs respond to challenging questions? Are all of the answers that you have only offered from their religious materials? Are you admonished continuously to accept things at face value and by blind faith?

Meet Mike in his own words:

On the night before he was crucified, Jesus was in the garden of Gethsemane wrestling intensely with what would happen the next day. It was Jesus' darkest hour. It was the point in his life that he was most alone, bitterly frightened, with no one to turn to. And he asked God to take the cup away that was waiting for him. And he began his prayer with the word, "Abba..." If you were following the story of redemption through the Bible to this point, it would be a word that would, in some respects, catch you quite off guard. "Abba" as a term of address, was one of real knowing, real relationship, and real intimacy. It's not really accurate to say it's the equivalent of 'daddy,' but the effect may be just as jarring, and to see it as almost 'daddy'-like, when you consider who those around Jesus knew their God - their heavenly Father - to be. He seemed very stern. Very wrathful. He seemed like someone you could never please. Punishing, almost.

He seemed much more interested in whether or not you were doing what He told you to do than in having any kind of loving father/child relationship. So it was almost like Jesus had a new portrait of God - of his Father - that he wanted to unveil to us. We were all with him in a gallery of sorts, and in front was a new work of art, which up to now had sat on an easel with a sheet draped over it. And Jesus walked up, and in a simple word of address - 'Abba' - pulled away the sheet, and all of a sudden we saw anew in the unveiled picture who God - who his Father - really was, and it wasn't at all what we expected.

My father passed away earlier this year. It's said that most of us get the views we have of God from the image of our fathers. In my own life, these two figures have played off each other in my own mind, with what I believed about my daddy influencing what I believed about God, and what I thought I believed about God impacting what I believed about my daddy. God, for a lot of people takes on a lot of the characteristics - good and bad - of the man who is initially the most dominant figure in our lives. For various reasons, there are exceptions to this, but it seems to be generally true, at least until the point where life challenges us to find a God of our own understanding.

My daddy was mostly a strict father. He was never, ever verbally or physically abusive - nothing like that - but it was clear he was in charge. And I sensed as a kid that what was playing out in my home was what played out in the story we read of Israel and its relationship to God in the Old Testament - that if they did what was wrong, they'd be punished, and if they did right, well, they just wouldn't be punished. That seemed to be the main rule of law on Lake Joy Road in Perry, GA, as I grew up.

And it only echoed and enforced what I heard as a kid about God, too. I grew up in a church of genuinely good-hearted people, but I am convinced few really thought on a deep level about what they were preaching to impressionable kids and teenagers about God. And honestly, when the typical Southern Baptist pastor is telling you every Sunday the typical heaven-vs-hell theology taught by your typical Southern Baptist Church, it's hard not to grow up with a very stern, and disappointed, and wrathful, and angry-all-the-time God.

At a very early age, religion, faith, and the church began to have a very big imprint in my life. My daddy didn't go with our family to church on Sundays. My momma would take my two sisters and me to Sunday School, and the 11 am church service every week, while daddy spent Sunday mornings working outside on our small farm. And as I got to the age where I was able to hear and begin to understand what was being taught in Sunday school and at church, I came to believe in no uncertain terms that my daddy would burn in hell 'forever and ever' when he died.

Religion, faith, and the church took ahold of me in a way very different from my friends. And I think I only recently came to understand why. At its most basic level, it was because my friends' families went to church together. And, as a result, none of them ever had to deal with the prospect of a parent burning in hell forever and ever. When you have a parent, who's facing that eternal prospect, these particular Christian doctrines become much more than words on thin, rustling pages turned in the pew on Sunday morning. It becomes a literal cross you carry in almost every waking moment. And if it doesn't, it sure as hell should.

I feared God. In a much, much different way, but oddly and in some ways the same, I also feared my Father. And I feared God for my Father. And so, for these reasons, I grew up with a God and a father who seemed a lot alike. The understanding of one had an impact on my perception of the other.

I went to inpatient rehab for my alcoholism for the first time in the mid-1990s. In every inpatient treatment center, there are a couple of days on the calendar of your stay when key members of your family are supposed to come in, and you're to address with them some of the root issues underlying your alcoholism and addiction. It's generally a very healing time for all family members and quite key to long-term recovery. But I didn't want momma and daddy coming out to do family therapy. I expected daddy to be angry, to be critical, and to be extremely disappointed in me if he were to find out his son was an alcoholic. I think our family as a whole kept from my daddy as best we could the truth that his son was an alcoholic, and that his son had spent a few weeks in rehab to deal with alcoholism.

But the alcoholism disease keeps very bad secrets. It's a beast that makes its own rules, and you follow them. And more wreckage and more destruction just happen as a symptom of the disease. And Daddy found out sometime later that I was an alcoholic.

And it's hard to even find the words to describe how a portrait of my daddy emerged that was so utterly and completely unlike the image of him that I had in my mind. My daddy turned out to be far different from the man I feared he was. Daddy spent the better part of the next twenty-five years being my biggest encourager, my biggest supporter, my best friend. He was the one - and in the recent years, really the only one - who chased me down in hotels, in jails, after lost jobs, in detox centers and rehabs. He never stopped telling me how much he believed in me. He told me shortly before he died that he had made a vow to himself that he was willing to give everything he owned to help me find peace, serenity, and sobriety. He would find me at my lowest, in my darkest hour, alone and frightened. And he would stoop down to where I was, and say, "Mike, what's continuing to beat you down is that you don't really know who you are. But I do. You don't know you like I know you. And I believe in you. And I believe in your gifts. And I believe in your heart. You can do this! Take my hand - let's get back up."

But a parallel miracle began to occur at the same time. My misunderstanding of who God really is started to disappear. God, too, spent the better part of the last twenty-five years encouraging me, supporting me, showing me he was a friend, chasing me down in hotels, in jails, after lost jobs, in detox centers and rehabs. God never stopped telling me how much he believed in me. God showed me more clearly how he had been willing to give everything necessary to help me find peace, and serenity, and sobriety. God would find me at my lowest, stoop down to where I was, and say, "Mike, what's continuing to beat you down is that you don't really know who you are. But I do. You don't know you like I know you. And I believe in you. And I believe in your gifts. And I believe in your heart. You can do this! Take my hand - let's get back up."

In AA, we have what we call 'paradoxes.' We surrender to win. We die to live. We only keep what we have by giving it away. I don't know whether or not this is a paradox, but in all of this, with my alcoholism, God walked over to the easel where the portrait of my daddy stood, with a covering over it, and God pulled it away so I could see who my daddy really was.

And in the same manner, my daddy walked over to the easel where the portrait of God stood, with a covering over it, and daddy pulled it away so I could see who God really is.

And if someone would have walked up to God after he had again come forward to forgive me and rescue me and encourage me and love me - if someone were to walk up to God and say, “Are you supposed to be doing this?”, God would have said, “What else could I do? He’s my child.”

And if someone had walked up to daddy after he had again for the hundredth time come forward to forgive me and rescue me and encourage me and love me - if someone were to have walked up to him and said, “Are you supposed to be doing this?”, daddy would have said, “What else could I do? He’s my son.”

And if anyone were to come up and ask me now, Mike, why are you able to face today all that life is tossing at you, when the hours again grow dark, and when you’re still very much alone, and when you're threatened by your own fear, why are you able to go out and face carrying your own cross day to day?

I would give two answers in one:

“What else could I do? I know who my Father is.”

CHAPTER 6 THE NOTION OF MORALITY: THERE'S NO RIGHT, NO WRONG, JUST SERVICE

> *"The nonexistence of God makes more difference to some of us than to others. To me, it means that there is no absolute morality, that moralities are sets of social conventions devised by humans to satisfy their needs."* Bertrand Russell

For centuries humankind has been addicted to chasing the delusion of morality. People expect you to have some sense of morality, which is why it is unfathomable when you see someone commit a heinous, cruel, or unthinkable crime. We define morality as conformity to ideals of right human conduct. Social mores insist upon the unanimous agreement concerning which behaviors are acceptable by the inhabitants of its society. These guidelines for proper behavior evolve to meet the needs of the time. I am willing to admit that, for the most part, people follow the laws of the social order in which they live either by choice or by avoidance of negative consequences.

Philosophers have argued for centuries on what is right or wrong human behavior. But morality in itself is an entirely human-made construct, so the argument will continue to evolve as man evolves. Ideas about morality have ranged from a mostly humane approach of engaging with your fellow man to the opposite end of the spectrum that encourages hedonism and selfish indulgence. The more philanthropic designs on living rest within the fibers of religious ideations. Buddhism has suggested we strive to obtain enlightenment through moral or ethical living, but who makes the rules and who decides what is moral or immoral? The subject of morality has been the meat upon which the likes of Aristotle, Immanuel Kant, and Thoreau devoted many an hour feasting on these ideas and questions.

It occurs to me that how humans would behave towards each other unencumbered by moral values or religious manipulation is the true morality if any exists at all. Furthermore, if God had intended for man to have a defined system of moral values, wouldn't those values have been incorporated into our DNA? For that matter, who is to say that they are not? Yet we are uncomfortable with the idea of allowing people to behave according to their natural inclinations. We fear what man's base nature will bring to light. Still, we successfully fail at the attempt to achieve a "moral life."

The rationale appears that without the social constructs of religion and other sets of moralistic codes, our behavior would mimic that of animals. But who's to say which set of ethics is the right set by which to live? Do we truly know if little Timmy would share his toys if not otherwise persuaded by mommy and daddy to do so? And should he have to share? My great-grandmother was married at the age of 13 and bore five children. She was born on January 13th, 1913, and at this time in history, her marriage was completely acceptable. Fast forward to 2020, and only four states have banned child marriage without exception: Minnesota, Pennsylvania, Delaware, and New Jersey. In Mississippi, it is acceptable to get married at the tender age of 10. I guess that many states have not bothered to amend these laws because it has become, for the most part, a non-issue.

Conversely, in most states, the legal age of consent to sexual relations range between 16-18 years old. Why is there such a disparity in the age to have sex and the age to get married? Does this make any sense at all? Morality appears to apply if and when it is convenient for the masses to address a particular subject.

Laws around prohibition and alcohol consumption have changed throughout the years and vary dramatically around the world. In Europe, it is common for children to imbibe in alcoholic beverages at the dinner table without a thought to their age. While we can make a myriad of arguments either for or against child drinking, whether the behavior is right or wrong rests purely in the mind of the individual and its societal norms. If you ask a teetotaler from the heart of the bible belt, they will rebuke such parents who would dare to partake in the devil's spirits and much less with their children.

The reality is that there is no such thing as right and wrong. People perceive issues to be right or wrong in the midst of a moral dilemma. The only thing that matters is how behavior does or does not serve you. Think about it. If a lie will keep you out of trouble with the law, will you tell it? If you were able to steal some food to feed your starving children, would you take it? If a burglar threatened the lives of your family and you had a gun in the home, would you shoot him to save your life and the lives of your family? In each of these cases, you can argue either for or against the action. One can reason that either action is moral or immoral based upon the circumstances and your point of view. The certainty is that as human beings, we will decide to do whatever we determine serves us best at the moment. And what you do at that moment is your true morality. You would have a jury of 12 to either agree or disagree that you made the right decision at that specific time. The vote would vary by the belief systems that drive each juror to make the "moral" decisions that they have embraced as a way of life.

The Law of Polarity tells us that everything is dual, has an opposite, and has poles. Examples of opposites are hot and cold or up and down. While everything may have its equal opposite, they are opposite poles of the same thing. When you think about right and wrong, they are both opposite sides of the same coin. This opposition brings the argument that opposites are identical, but vary in degree. Duality is somewhat different from polarity in that each pole has the essence of its opposite within it. How you decide to view a situation may also be relative. While you may think it feels uncomfortably hot in here, I may think that it feels toasty and warm. How you perceive a situation might be entirely different from how another person views the same event. It is the possibility of the difference in perspective that disavows rules that define morality.

The ability to create exceptions to every rule creates the biggest fallacy in religion. There is no scenario in the universe where every person would follow their faith to the letter in every circumstance. It is impossible. We all know this, so why have we sustained the flawed views of faith and the pseudo-morality that it requires? Why do we all strive to pursue the futile possibility of becoming perfect or better people? And if becoming "better" is the goal, who determines what better is and what it looks like for everyone? Is it possible to be perfect just the way you are? Wow!!! Now that's a thought. What if the way you are living right now is your highest self? What if you have a satisfying life experience by panhandling enough money each day to support your beer habit and have enough to eat? What if being a stripper pays the bills, makes you feel good about yourself and puts you and your kids through college? What if you are the best booster in the Tri-City area and steal enough to provide for yourself and your family? Are these people "bad" people? Do we have the right to judge their motives?

The laws of the land define legal and illegal for us. But the laws change according to those in power. Once upon a time, it was illegal for black people to enter white only restrooms —my how times appear to have changed. Religious ideologies define our morality, yet they provide loopholes of exclusion and options for forgiveness. However, it is the spiritual law and laws of nature that govern all absolutely without judgment or prejudice. The universal mind makes no distinction between right or wrong; only consequences. And when we make our own decisions about what is right or wrong for us, those very same consequences should be the only thing that influences how we make our decisions. What goes up must come down, so says the law of gravity.

Without the benefit of language, culture, or education, the universe provides the laws and guidelines that teach us how to live; what serves or does not serve us. Your soul is naturally in tune with these laws, but our lives have been heavily influenced by religious beliefs that have misshapen our inherent "knowingness" of how to exist in the world. If you consider things in a completely unbiased manner, you will notice that all of the things that you cannot do, you cannot do. Equally true is the notion that something that you should not do have negative consequences. I get it that that may sound strange, but the things that we intrinsically cannot do are already beyond our capabilities.

For example, we cannot live underwater without some form of breathing apparatus. We cannot fly without the benefit of technology that would allow us to soar briefly in the skies. We cannot propagate our species by sex with animals. We cannot create life out of anything (although we do our best to play God through manipulating stem cells and cloning.) And please note that even though our technologies have allowed us to circumvent some of our limitations, there are severe consequences should we have any misstep in executing that technology. If the plane crashes, we will almost certainly perish. If your scuba gear runs out of oxygen, you will drown, etc. Beyond the limitations that the universe has set upon us all, the sky is the limit.

The universal law of cause and effect suggests that there are always consequences for every decision made, be the outcomes desirable or undesirable.

Questions surrounding so many facets of our way of existence are naturally addressed by nature and the universe. Natural or Universal laws like the Law of Karma, Law of Cause and Effect, Law of Attraction, and others impact everyone and bring consequences for our actions regardless of belief in their existence. Later on, I will talk more about some of those laws that have been discovered through time to demonstrate the universe's ultimate control over all living things. Natural is defined as being based on an inherent sense of right and wrong or occurring in conformity with the ordinary course of nature. Somehow, we have collectively bought into the idea that our natural state is not good enough to support a civilized standard of living.

Let's look a little closer at the idea of monogamy, for instance. Now I cannot, in my truth, sit here and tell you that I have never considered slitting a tire or putting some sugar in a gas tank in a jealous rage in my lifetime. And I have a few visible scars from jealous lovers from my past. But the question is, is it natural to insist that an individual remain faithful to you and you alone-forever? The facts suggest a reality that is far from the idealistic dream of a romantic happily ever after. In fact, according to the infidelity statistics, about 40% of unmarried relationships and 25% of marriages see at least one infidelity incident. An issue of Marriage and Divorce journal also stated that 70% of all Americans engage in some kind of affair sometime during their marital life.

Yet we continue to get married (I'm on my third marriage.) Do we require a certain amount of denial to function in our society and keep things going in this farce we call civilization? Someone accused me of being an absolutist because I see that our system of false morality does not work overall. He suggests that if a high enough percentage of the system works, a certain amount of error or failure is acceptable. To make an exception to the rule seems to be the modus operandi of the world. ***But I say, if the world is not black and white, then the devil is in the grey areas.***

Everything that exists in the world exists because it is a possibility. This concept is difficult to digest because, in our self-righteousness, we feel that only the opportunities of which we approve should exist. Serial killers, rapists, pedophiles, homeless, drug addicts, thieves, prostitutes, drug dealers, pornographers, sex traffickers, and every other "deviant" lifestyle choice exists. Remember the law of polarity. They exist because their opposites exist. So in effect, we have created our own demons. In nature, there are bugs, buzzards, lice, fleas, ticks, mosquitos, flies, bacteria, cancer, and a thousand other unpleasant beings that we do not appreciate but serve a purpose in perpetuating life on this planet.

You do not know good unless evil exists, and evil is in the eye of the beholder. The people that you consider evil are a by-product of what occurs when you force people to succumb to a sense of morality that does not hold true to them. They act in ways that produce abhorrent deeds against humanity. In societies that teach freedom of sexuality, and encourage free sexual expression, you do not see cases of sexual crimes. In communities that provide for all of its members, you do not see theft and crime occurrences. It is when we create wealth that we create poor and the consequences that follow. We don't often want to admit it, but we have, indeed, created our own demons.

You may ask, "Are you saying that rapists and pedophiles are ok?" I would answer with a resounding "No!" And should I encounter any number of the above-listed deviants, I would have angst and concern about their proximity to my family or me. That said, they all have the right to exist because of the possibility of their existence. And I have to believe that they each serve some purpose in the cycle of life in the universe. They have always existed in the world and will continue to remain in the future so long as we continue to create the possibility of their existence. Without yin, there is no yang. Without sadness, we would not know happiness. After all, according to Einstein, it's all relative. If the story of Adam and Eve were true, would they have known they were in a paradise and appreciate the garden if they never got put out? That's where it all supposedly started, right? This idea of choice, free will, and all that?

So, can I give you some good news? Or at least provide a glimmer of hope for a more palatable future? Your morality is your own and of your design exclusively and individually. The truth is you make your own rules as you go. You use what you learn from each experience to create your morality for the future. You determine what serves you at all times. You may not get it right every time, but there is no such thing as getting it wrong. It is all experience, and experience is your unmitigated purpose for being. You get to decide for yourself what values are essential to your soul's well-being. This is why you may make one decision for this event and decide upon another course of action for the same event in the future.

You can only be genuinely comfortable by living your truth of morality. If your soul wants to experience the world as a transgender person, you cannot be at peace trying to live by a moral code incongruent with your soul's desires. And as with any choice you make about how you choose to live your life, your soul is only subject to the consequences that the law of cause and effect provides, whether desirable or undesirable. For example, if living a queer lifestyle in a small town of people who are intolerant of such lifestyles, one may have to deal with the inequities, prejudices, and mistreatment of others. It is then your choice to either deal with the disapproval of others, move to an area that is more acquiescent, fight for your rights, or hide your true self. Either way, the choice is yours. You cannot force others to accept your truth, no more than they have the right to deny yours. There are only choices: no right, no wrong, just service.

Any concrete moral standard that has been created by others sets value systems that are unachievable by all in every circumstance. Whenever there are exceptions to a rule, in my opinion, a rule is rendered null and void. So, it is pointless to try to live by anyone's moral code but your own. You create your system as you go. Do your very best to live up to your sense of highest self. Any thing other than accepting this truth is to live in the denial and hypocrisy upon which all religions, laws, and social mores demand. It's sort of like helping a friend's child continue to believe in Santa Claus when you know "good in hell well" that it is a lie. Walking in your truth is the only way to live in true freedom of self. You will find that honest living, in this way, will strip away the chains of guilt, blame, and shame, which are not natural states of being; they are learned behaviors. The feelings are instilled into you from birth and perpetuated and reinforced throughout life until you die. These feelings are all a veiled attempt at controlling human behavior.

Because of the shared delusion of false morality, the lies that we weave to support these myths serve an all-consuming need to preserve a fictitious identity. We end up lying about everything and to everyone. More importantly, the havoc these lies wreak has their most damaging effect on the one person we have to preserve- ourselves. Within the web of these lies, we lose connection with our internal compass that should lead us to a fulfilling life. Our souls provide the compass that enables us to navigate this world successfully. But we have been conditioned to ignore that voice. "Don't trust your instincts"; "just do as we say". "Follow the rules." "Keep your head down." "Fly under the radar." "Don't rock the boat." Need I go on? Can you think of a few more stupid euphemisms that we blindly adhere to in a mundane effort to keep up appearances?

Morality is a human-made construct that is unsustainable and, by default, dooms us to a life of bitterness and regret. Within these webs, rest the seeds of self-doubt and uncertainty that lead to even greater addictions beyond the addiction to religion. Alcoholism, drug addiction, food addiction, and the like are false gods that we pray to for salvation from the inner conflict we have created under the weight of the inability to keep our lies going. The weight is crushing and destructive. They say that pressure will burst a pipe, and we see our pipes break in various ways in our lives. We get caught in adulterous affairs that cost us our families, our possessions, and our reputations. We commit suicide when the fear of what lies on the other side becomes less frightening than the idea of waking up to another day of the living hell of our lives. We swallow and inject poison into our bodies to numb the excruciating pain of our benign existence. And we avoid our realities by spending all of our emotional coins on futile experiences like work, sex, or hours at the gym.

And to be clear, I am not suggesting that we become 100% honest about everything and leave trails of hurt feelings in our wake as we trample through everyone we stumble upon in our lives. Let them eat cake! I am suggesting that we take an approach of self-preservation that allows us to walk in our truth. Who decided that we all have to pretend to like things that we hate to protect someone else's feelings? Why do I have to pretend to be something that I am not for you to love and accept me? Why do I have to swallow my opinions and take yours as my own when I know I don't agree? And how long do I have to pretend NOT to notice all of the hypocrisy of all of these supposedly Christian people who party with me on Saturday night, but show up all shiny and new on Sunday morning? I mean, really? I'm just supposed to ignore the fact that this preacher who was having sex with all these young boys is a hypocrite? How often are we supposed to "forgive" the "Good Reverend" for falling into the temptation of a young woman who is not his wife? We have to get past all of the pretenses at some point.

Next Steps and Takeaways from this chapter:

The Debate: Is right and wrong determined by your actions or your beliefs?

The fact is that the "Good Reverend" or the Priest or any other religious leader, for that matter, is only human just like me. They can't live a "righteous" life 24/7 anymore than I can. So why bother with all of the pretenses? Let's do the best we can to make the best choices for ourselves in each moment. Learn from what we decide are mistakes that do not demonstrate our vision of self and move on to bigger and better things. I challenge you to assess yourself and identify the areas in which you are not honest with yourself first and then with the world. What are you pretending to be or not be to appear as a moral or upright person? Do you have some weird sexual fetish that you are ashamed of being revealed to others? Do you smoke or drink and don't want your friends or family to know that you hit the "sticky icky" every day or from time to time? Do you hate your boss? Are knowingly sleeping with someone's significant other or cheating on your own significant other?

Speak your truth to yourself. Then evaluate how those things that you have defined as immoral either serve or not serve your highest good. What are the potential consequences of the behaviors that you engage in on this list? If you can live in peace with the results, then you are fine. If you cannot, then you might consider making some personal changes.

My grandmother used to say, "Every tub has to sit on its own bottom." Only you can define what is right or wrong for you. In the bible, the Apostle Paul said in I Corinthians 10:23,

"All things are lawful for me, but all things are not expedient: all things are lawful for me, but all things edify not."

He even knew that there is no such thing as right and wrong, only those that serve your highest good or not.

The reality is that there will never be universal peace, universal good, or an end to world hunger. God designed a world of possibilities. Without relativity, you cannot know yourself, and neither can God know itself. You cannot know peace without war. You cannot know joy without pain. You cannot know happiness without sadness. The universal mind knows itself through each experience that you and everyone else in the world has. ***You cannot create something without creating the possibility of its opposite equal.*** It is what it is.

Meet Randolph in his own words:

Basically, I grew up in the Pentecostal, Apostolic, and COGIC background all my life. My Grandparents founded the church, but my grandmother was the matriarch of both the church and the family. She had eight children, and they were the first members of the church. From day one, they were the founding members involved in the care and running of the church: they were the choir, devotion leaders, members, etc. I was born in the church, where I was a musician, the drummer. My mother's philosophy was you were either going to do this shit, or your ass is grass-and that's a quote! My mother said I needed to play like God was watching. I am so grateful for that because today, I am an outstanding drummer. I was always trained mentally not to challenge God's word. But yet we read scriptures that God used so many other things like donkeys or cocks crowing and so many other things to speak to us in addition to human beings to get his point across. God talked to Noah and told him it was going to rain, but even a slug got on the ship, and all of the animals were obedient. So, these scriptures can't be the only way to talk to God. So why would God be confined to just what King James wrote? Who is this motherfucker anyway? Fast forward in my life until my grandmother died on June 12th, 1995. It's like that movie Big momma's house and everything fell apart. Everything changed. Then I developed a resentment against God. We were going to church almost every day of the week. Then everybody started coming out of the closet doing everything that we knew to be a sin. I wondered to myself is any of this church stuff for real? So, then my quest began where I was questioning God. With all of these fake people around me, like what the fuck is this shit really about?

About 2001-2002, I was cool with the church again but was getting high on drugs. I used to go to my grandmother's grave high on cocaine and start cursing the grave about all of the things going wrong in the church. But God spoke to me in an audible voice and said to me,

"Greater things shall You do.' The voice did coincide with scripture, so it felt authentic. But I continued to get heavily into drugs. At one point, I thought I heard the bells to the upper room during a damn near drug overdose.

One day I was all geeked up and thinking about God. I was always a spiritual person, no matter what. But at the same time, I didn't really believe in hell. I felt that God was really a loving God. Why would he send you to hell? So, one day, I wrote down the word enemy: the enemy comes to kill, steal, and destroy. I wrote it over and over. God made me play with the words. Then I switched the letters to say enter-me instead of enemy. Then I realized that I allowed something to enter me that was controlling me, and it was the drugs. I was still on my journey to try to find God.

In 2012, I entered the AA rooms for the first time and discovered my God. It was like telling the slaves they were free. And not only are you free, but I am giving all of this shit to you. I was like, am I really free. In the church, you are ruled by all of these ideologies, rules, and regulations. So, it was a new beginning to understand the nature of my own true God. On November 20th, 2015, I realized we have the God of Abraham, Isaac, and Jacob, and then you have the God of me and everyone else in AA.

Now I realize that I am a God within my own right. I am still a Christian—"Father, Son, and Holy Ghost" for life. Remember where Jesus said that he thought it not robbery to make himself equal with God? And we are heirs of Christ, so that makes me equal with God. And from my wife, I am learning about the law of attraction which is now an important part of my reality.

CHAPTER 7 ARE SPIRITUAL LEADERS EXPLOITING US OR ARE THEY NECESSARY?

> *"With religion, I was always like, does it matter if it's true if it makes you happy?" Matt Stone*

Another of the fundamental imperfections in religion is its reliance upon its human leaders who, by virtue of being human, are flawed. Apart from this is the idea of "working on ourselves" to achieve salvation, enlightenment, heaven's pearly gates, or whatever promise your religion offers. We have to learn how to work on ourselves from flawed individuals. So then, what is work? Webster defines work as physically or mentally exerting oneself, especially in sustained effort or continuous repeated operations. So, pause—can you think of five pieces of "work" that your religion requires from you to be, to achieve, to receive, or to believe something? Are you challenged to aspire, to become, to overcome, to resist, to pray, to have faith, to trust, to obtain approval, to receive forgiveness, to receive your reward, to be healed, or to be successful? And what of the peddlers of these ideas? What skin, if any, do they have in the game? What is their responsibility to their believers? Is their authority God-given? And if so, how were they "chosen"?

To answer these questions, let's first define what it means to be a leader. A leader is a person who commands a group, organization, or country. Your priest, guru, yogi, pastor, bishop, minister, reverend, nun, or whichever title you provide is someone to whom you give authority over your soul. My question would be, "Why would I ever give anyone authority over my existence?" Yet we do. We willingly give them access to the most fundamental and intimate resources that we possess—our money, our children, our business, our happiness, and, most importantly, our trust. Is there any human being in whom we should trust with such riches? Should they be allowed access to our most vulnerable places, and if so, what do they owe us in return for such liberty?

We are taught nearly from birth, not to think for ourselves. In school, we learn society's versions of facts and history. Our parents force their points of view of the world upon us, and they admonish us to honor our elders. Critical thought is discouraged, so we learn to "do as we are told." So, it is no wonder that our perceptions of the world are wrought with conflicts when what we feel or know as right inside does not match what they tell us is correct. Still, how can we learn from our elders that which we need to know to formulate our ideas and discover our truths?

It would take an entire book to recount examples of where such leaders have failed its constituents throughout history. But what is the impetus that continues to drive us to seek out spiritual leaders to govern our souls? Do we need them? And if so, for what purpose do they serve us? Here I will share my elucidation of how spiritual leaders can positively help us. But make no mistake, I am in no way suggesting that you have to have one to be spiritually whole. There is nothing more harmful and hurtful than a spiritual leader or other people of authority that will take advantage of you in an area that you are most spiritually vulnerable. But ultimately, it is YOUR responsibility to guard your heart in these matters. "I didn't know" is not an option for the universe. You are subject to the spiritual law of cause and effect by the choices and decisions you make for your life. So, let's take a look at what these potential leaders can or should mean to us.

Religious Leaders

You may find it odd that I place religious leaders first on my list in this segment. However, I do so with the understanding that while many of you may be searching for answers, most of you will still choose to remain within your chosen religion. You have every right to do so, and I would never encourage you to do anything differently than what your soul desires. Your soul may be quite content to attend a church or a mosque or a temple. I only admonish you to use discretion and due diligence when choosing the governor of your soul. You must safeguard your possessions, your money, and your children against those who might not have your best interests at heart.

It is your responsibility to protect yourself and your loved ones. You cannot be excused for having blind trust in someone simply because of their title. The universe does not protect against naivete. The universal laws apply whether you are ignorant of them or not. Trust the intuition that shows you how you feel about the experiences that you have under a spiritual leader's care. If something feels amiss, that is your universal compass alerting you that you are not going the right way. Do not ignore those signals. Leave, or at the very least investigate at once. To coin a tired old phrase, it is better to be safe than sorry. Likewise, no one can scam you without your willing participation. The serial killer Dennis Rader, also known as BTK, was a Cub Scout leader and President of the church council at Christ Lutheran Church where he was a member. He was accused of ten murders in his killing spree. None of the church members had any inkling that there was a serial killer among them working with their children.

Most importantly, if you choose to stay within a specific faith, your leader should fully exemplify the ideals of that faith to the best of his or her ability. It will become complicated for you to continue to follow leadership if you have discovered that they live a duplicitous life that is contrasting with their teachings. Wherever there are exceptions to the rule, the rule is no more valid but rather a suggestion or possibility. After reading this book, blatant hypocrisy should no longer be comfortable for you. It used to disturb me, but I now know that I alone am responsible for the people I entrust with my heart.

If I find that a leader's life hardly reflects the teachings that they claim to believe, I simply do not follow their guidance. They are impoverished in many ways, have constant chaos and havoc in their lives, and are not very happy. Judgment permeates their attitudes toward others. In the case of some supposed Christian leaders, I do not see any glimpse of how Jesus lived in their lives; I hear only religious rhetoric. But many religious leaders do their best to live by the standards their religions require, and their faith has served them very well in many ways. You have to decide for yourself what path to take to find wholesome leadership after much reflection and searching of your soul.

Guide

Everything that we need to survive and exist in the universe is already inside of us. However, we have learned through institutions of civilization, such as religion, education, and laws, to ignore our intuition's inner leadings. It is similar to caging a lion who is the natural king of the jungle. He is now confined to a zoo environment. He is not allowed to develop its instincts from the wild. It is still a lion, but it has been handicapped and trained to exist in captivity. Many, if not all, domesticated lions would fail to thrive if they had to suddenly return into the wild and the survival of the fittest framework of life in the safari. Likewise, as human beings, since we have not been taught to live by our natural instincts, we can benefit from the teaching of people who have gained experience in the ways of spiritual expression and expansion.

A guide is one who advises or shows the way to others. Meditation is an example of a skill that one might benefit from having a guide to understand how to maximize the meditation experience fully. A spiritual guide can help you push past the desire to give up or succumb to the illusion of problems in the natural world. They can help you grow your ability to successfully overcome the effects of life traumas and move towards spiritual healing. A guide is not higher than you; they simply have more experience in a particular subject than you. Use your intuition when choosing a guide for your spiritual growth in a specific area. It is both helpful for you and the guide. Teaching another sharpens the skills of the guide in their area of expertise.

Mentors

One can benefit from having mentors in every aspect of our lives. I would only caution everyone who looks for such mentors to be very discerning and intentional about whomever you choose. Please remember, above all things, that these are only people just like you and me. There can be people for whom you have the utmost respect, and for those who have earned it, you may even have some form of deference or even reverence. But with that said, they are human just like you.

This person should have already accomplished what you wish to achieve. They should guide you through both the pitfalls and the benefits of the journey they took to get there. This person is only an example of the possibilities that you can achieve and, thus, not the end-all and be all. Your development and growth should not depend upon their approval or disapproval of your actions. They should not insist on telling you what to do but encourage you to discover your path to what you hope to achieve. Refrain from putting anyone on a pedestal because any faith you have in them could be tainted if you see them make a mistake.

Confidante

It is vital to have someone to confide your deepest secrets, hurts, and traumas. You must choose to do so with someone who can provide a safe environment for you to unburden your soul. You cannot be healthy and live your best life if you are holding on to the past's unhealed pains. Suppose you are unable to release them by yourself through meditation and spiritual work. In that case, it can be constructive to secure a person of great life experience that can help you process those feelings productively. I am very selective about entrusting anyone with my most private thoughts or concerns. But there are moments where it is necessary to have a sounding board upon which I can bounce ideas or thoughts that I am unable to reconcile within myself immediately. There is no shame in seeking help or guidance from another who has more experience than yourself within a specific area of life. I am reminded of the phrase "there is more room out than in." Find that particular person that will allow you to be your most vulnerable and naked if that is what you need to heal.

"You are only as sick as your secrets." This is a common euphemism that one might hear in the rooms of Alcoholics Anonymous. You must have someone you can confide that will give you guidance based upon sound experience rather than personal opinion. Your internal compass, your soul, knows what you desire. Any advice that you receive should resonate with a sense of peace within your soul. This is not to be confused with having your ego assuaged by hearing what you want to hear. There is a big difference. Most often, we ask questions to which we already know the answers. You may often look for validation and approval for what you feel or desire inside. Trust your instincts, but do not be afraid to hear a different perspective that will allow clarity when you are too close to a situation to see it objectively.

Model

Imagination is one of the beautiful gifts that we possess as humans being. "If your mind can conceive it, you can achieve it" as they so often say. But what if you are lost and unsure how to realize your full potential? Or what if you have an inkling about what you believe spiritually but can't entirely devise the framework of your beliefs. Models are fundamental to your success because the simple truth is, "you can't be what you can't see." It is not even necessary for you to personally know a model. It is very much ok to admire them from afar. A model is an illustration of specific attributes that you hope to manifest within yourself, not the definition. If you want to immerse yourself in meditation fully, you can look to people like Deepak Chopra, who is an expert in meditation.

If you see someone like Iyanla Vanzant or the Dalai Lama, for example, who exemplifies qualities you want to develop within yourself, feel free to borrow and emulate those attributes. Allow yourself to aspire to whatever level of greatness that you desire. If you are diligent in your intentions, the universe will open the door for you to fulfill the destiny that you genuinely wish. But you can only achieve the highest goal that you can visually see. So, there is a massive benefit to having a model beyond your reach. In doing so, you extend the reach of your imagination. Seeing a model live your dream reinforces your faith that you can achieve the goals you set for yourself. Do not be afraid to aim high because only your imagination can limit your ambition.

Next Steps and Takeaways from this chapter:

The Debate: Should you forgive religious leaders who fail their followers by breaking the law or immoral transgressions that they preach against in their teachings?

This book is designed to provide you with insight, additional color, and opportunities to assess your current religious beliefs and values. You will also evaluate how you engage with the leaders who facilitate your spiritual practices or life views. Do you have a leader, mentor, role model, or confidante in your life that provides you the care, collaboration, and confidentiality that allows you to feel safe and supported? If not, open your mind to exploring opportunities that you may not have been open to in the past. Research people online who have accomplished the things you want to achieve. Open your mind to other religions if you choose to follow religion and look for ideas that may help you to define or to develop yourself.

I study several religions not to seek to join their organization, but for best practices that can help me to grow personally. I do not belong to an individual church. I am still quite open to attending a seminar, religious service, or convention that discusses spiritual practices or ideas that I am exploring for my growth. I am so open to going to an event hosted by Deepak Chopra. I would do cartwheels to have the opportunity to meet the Dalai Lama!!! I am open to everything and attached to nothing; thus, I am giving myself a cornucopia of avenues of growth and experiences.

Meet Jay in his own words:

Religion has always been an interesting thing for me. I grew up in the African Methodist Episcopal Church (AME), a very ritualistic sect of Christianity. We had so many rituals similar to those of the Catholic Church like communion, and songs. But this belief gave me thoughts of a world beyond this one, which was terrifying. I often thought of the flames of hell consuming me, which is very torturous to a child. The monster under the bed had nothing on 'my heavenly father' just waiting to punish me for my sins. Another issue I never could get around was the lack of proof. I have always been a skeptic by nature, and I question everything. In short, out of all the religions throughout history, how could you be sure yours is correct? You can't be. You can only choose to ignore reality and have blind and biased faith. I grew out of that in my teen years and have not looked back. In my opinion, it is the uncertainty of the afterlife and our origin that troubles so many people and is why religion will never go extinct.

This does not make it real, however. Everyone must make peace with the who, what, when, where, why, and how of life on their own. This is a sad reality of life, but clinging to stories is not how I choose to deal with such an existential dilemma.

CHAPTER 8 WITHDRAWAL SYMPTOMS

> *"Religion is like drugs; it destroys the thinking mind." George Carlin*

George Carlin was a well-known atheist, and he had no qualms about voicing his opinion of religion. He was brought up in an Irish-Catholic home and attended a Roman Catholic high school. Yet we all know from his comedy that subsequently, his views about religion would morph into a total denunciation of his beliefs. He frequently vocalized in his standup acts how he ultimately rejected all religion, assuming a somewhat cynical view of those who "believe." So, it begs the question: What if, just what if all of the world's religions are not what they say they are? What if religion has been the Santa Claus that you never wanted to find out wasn't real? What now? What if the answer is that you just—don't—know? Somehow, we have collectively bought into the idea that our natural state is not good enough to support a civilized standard of living through the invention of religion, philosophy, and human laws.

We have subsequently replaced our divine intuition with the facts, history, and logic of other men. Therefore, in an entirely futile effort, we have accepted all of these rules—a false sense of morality—that we have decided that everyone in our society must live by to be an upstanding human being. Yet, no one lives these morals and values entirely, nor can they. And since we are not "naturally" perfect, various men throughout our history have searched for an ideal plan for the salvation of humanity through multiple religions. Now I am certainly not saying that we do not benefit from order, civilization, and human laws. However, the pretense about who we are creates anguish in many of us. This angst manifests in many inopportune and objectionable ways. Let's call them withdrawal symptoms.

For some people who come from an environment deeply rooted in religion, the ability to reject these ideas and walk away at the age of maturity is a simple process. They simply grow up and have a strong enough sense of self-identity to decide for themselves that a religious lifestyle does not mesh with their internal sense of self. They gain this awareness when they go through an abject immersion into another way of life that shows a different way of living than their upbringing. An example would be going away to college, where you are now in an environment that fosters the exploration of questions, different points of view, and freedom to think for self. Or maybe you join the military and get to travel the world and see alternative ways of life that offer possibilities you could never have imagined. But for those of us who struggle with letting go of the old and challenging the new, this can be a complicated process.

Withdrawal symptoms are the abnormal physical or pychological features that follow the abrupt discontinuation of a drug that has the capability of producing physical or mental dependence. When you attempt to break away by leaving your religion, rejecting your faith, or having a sense of failing your religion somehow, the cognitive dissonance that can happen within your now shattered identity can invoke a cornucopia of adverse events in your life. Cognitive dissonance occurs when a person holds two or more contradictory beliefs, ideas, or values; or participates in an action against one of these three and experiences psychological stress because of that.

For example, if you have always learned that it is a sin to have premarital sex, you may experience guilt and shame attached to the action when it occurs. It's akin to hearing from a parent or caregiver that you are ugly all of your life. Then you grow up, and someone attempts to compliment you by suggesting that you are pretty or that you are handsome. There is an inner conflict that happens when you hear a contradictory message from the ugliness message that you have heard from the most critical person in your world. It becomes difficult to receive the compliment. You will struggle to believe the praise. You may desperately want to embrace the compliment, but the struggle internally is a force to be reckoned with indeed.

So, let's use the framework of religion to flesh out this idea. You may not have considered the possibility of withdrawal from religion as a possibility. But maybe some of these example withdrawal symptoms may reverberate with you in some way. A few ways that withdrawal symptoms may show up for you are feelings of rebellion, guilt and shame, vulnerability, low self-esteem and self-doubt, and need for approval and acceptance.

In this chapter, we will explore these symptoms and try to identify the root cause and, hopefully, a solution for overcoming the effects of these problems to regain control of your sense of self-worth. I told you to prepare yourself for finding answers that you never thought you would have to consider. I hope that you will benefit from all of the soul searching that I had to undergo to reach these conclusions for myself. If you find that you do indeed suffer from the effects of one of these concerns, there is good news. Awareness is half of the solution to finding relief.

"We suffer from the maladies of the soul in total oblivion to their existence save for the pain that we endure trying to shoulder the burden of the distress." K.D.Foy

Rebellion

Let's first examine the issue of rebellion, which can be the most identifiable and relatable symptom. Rebellion is the action or process of resisting authority, control, or convention. The convention of religion is a designed belief in a supreme being or higher power that provide the rubrics for living or explaining the reason for your existence. If the belief system that you are exposed to does not mesh with your desire to express yourself, it is common to want to act out in defiance of the rules. This symptom can show up in the form of teenage runaways, suicide, and drug and alcohol abuse.

Were you the teenager who "wild' ed" out, "turned up", got pregnant, did drugs, or snuck out despite your parent's strict rules and disapproval? Do you know a PK son who got addicted to drugs or a daughter who married a drug dealer? Were you a Caucasian son or daughter who dated the African American guy or black girl despite your family's overt racism? These are all acts of rebellion. And whenever a rule or suggestion goes against your soul's belief system, acting out is one way of demonstrating your disdain for control over your behavior. Unfortunately, in many cases, acts of rebellion are the most destructive to one's self and have very little, if any, impact on the establishment from which you rebel. Hence, resistance is not so much an expression of your true feelings; you wouldn't want to be addicted to drugs after all. As teenagers, youth are not equipped with the maturity, experience, and foresight to see the danger of their rebellious choices. In youthful naivete, it may seem fun and exciting to rebel against the rules imposed on you.

Guilt and Shame

Guilt is one of the most powerful human emotions known to a man despite the reality that guilt is mostly a man-manufactured concept. You do not naturally feel guilty. You learn to have feelings of guilt or remorse resulting from disappointing either someone you respect, such as a parent or caregiver or yourself. Children will snatch their favorite toy away from a playmate and feel absolutely no remorse about it. It is the parent who teaches the child that the behavior is unacceptable. Mom makes you feel bad for disappointing her or for taking a cookie after she said no. Your wife caught you looking at another woman's big juicy butt, so you feel bad for betraying her trust (and for getting caught!). Almost everybody uses guilt as a weapon in some shape or form to manipulate, control, or diminish another person. A coach, "You let the team down." Or a grandmother, "I'm very disappointed in you." Shame began with Adam and Eve after eating the forbidden fruit in the garden, realizing they were naked, and then they were ashamed. This is most likely not a true story.

Children love to be naked. We teach them to have shame and disdain for their bodies. I mean afterall, we were all born naked, so why should God care what we wear or don't wear? Guilt and shame together are a powerful combo that packs a mean wallop when used effectively. Throw in the terror of burning in hell forever, and you have quite a principal instrument of dominance over the weak and the willing. Feelings of guilt and shame make you want to do one thing: hide. You have to protect your cigarettes, your darkest secrets, sexuality, your true beliefs, your trauma, your feelings, and on and on. Religious organizations capitalize on this guilt and shame, and their rules serve one main objective-fixing you because you are innately wrong. Your thoughts are wrong, your deeds are sinful, your desires are wrong, and only religion can fix you. If you are always wrong no matter what you do, this sense of hopelessness can create numerous opportunities to disappoint God, your family, your religious leaders, and, more importantly, yourself.

There is the slim hope of reaching the virtual carrot that religion offers, but no matter which religion you choose, very few get the carrot. Maybe, and I mean maybe, it will all work out if you get forgiven, or you are dead and finally get to go to heaven, reach enlightenment, or manage to be good enough. But tragically, for some religions, if you don't get it right this time, you have to do it all over again, and it might just be in the form of a lower life form.

Vulnerability

This brings me to the subject of vulnerability. It is the quality or state of being exposed to being attacked or harmed, either physically or emotionally. Because the religion has told you that you are wrong, you are now open to the following symptoms that are attached to your vulnerability: a new, more accepting religion, seeking love and approval from a potentially harmful person, drugs and alcohol to manage the guilt and shame of never being good enough, suicide because it's all so hopeless, reckless promiscuity, and I am sure you can add a few to this very abbreviated list. Ask yourself if this vulnerability is fair to the believer? Furthermore, if you have been conditioned your whole life that you as an individual are inherently flawed, you become open to seeking approval for your existence outside of yourself. So, when some charismatic manipulator presents themselves and offers validation to you, you can easily succumb to their influence. (Refer back to the chapter on cults.)

Next Steps and Takeaways from this Chapter:

The Debate: Are religious holy texts still relevant thousands of years later, or should religion evolve with time?

One of the most healing things that you can do for yourself is to find, heal, and rebuild your sense of self-worth and power. Know that you are enough just the way that you are, and you do not need outside validation to be okay. Approval from others can be desired and even appreciated, but should not be required. If you can determine the morals and values that are meaningful to you as an individual, you can set the tone for presenting yourself to others.

Your presentation of self to the world should not be out of rebellion, desperation, or deception to please others. Your brand should be defined from the inside and developed by the knowledge that you seek out for yourself. Validation should come from your soul's reaction to situations that you are presented with throughout your life. Nobody can tell you what is right or best for you. If their input affects you adversely within your soul, choose to ignore it. You are born to experience this world as God being you. I know this may sound corny, but you are a derivative of God in living color. Your expression is God's expression and therefore, cannot be wrong. You know what they say, "God didn't make no junk." Remember that golden nugget?

Meet Cornae in her own words:

Growing up as a little girl, I was brought up in the church. My foundation is COGIC. The Grand ole Church of God in Christ. I come from generations of Pastors, Bishops, Missionaries, Evangelists, and the list goes on. I learned really quickly that there were lots of dos and don'ts. Women were to dress a certain way. Dresses and skirts below the knee, stockings, slips, no tight dresses or skirts, no pants, or shorts. Makeup was at a minimum and very modest. We were taught that the men were the head of the household, and women were to be submissive to their husbands. It was definitely a boy's club. Most churches, revivals, and meetings were run by the men of the church. My father was a Pastor of Shekinah Glory COGIC. I loved my church. Serving under my dad and mom, I learned a lot. I always had a love for children. I became a Sunday school teacher and the choir director. Oh, did I forget to mention God gave me a beautiful voice to sing for him?

Over the years, growing up in the church was really exciting and tested my faith. I learned there are different cliques in the church. The church scene is small, and everyone knows everyone. I learned that with every title that you hold comes with great responsibility. (money) My gift began to make room for me, and I started to sing at different church programs, etc. My relationship with God became closer, and I gave my life to him.

Then came all the rules. No cussing, sex, smoking, drinking, dancing, only listen to gospel music, no boyfriends, and the list goes on. I began to read the BIBLE to see if all these rules were in there. Some were, some were not. Sometimes we just listen to people, but we don't do the research ourselves. We all pretty much know right from wrong. My experiences in the church world have been good and bad. Some people feel that they are better than you or you are beneath them.

The church scene has changed some say for the better, and some people are just set in their ways. I can say that the dress code has changed, and it's a lil more lax for men and women. Even the way we worship God. The music has changed because this world has changed. I believe that my generation and the younger generation just have a different and new way to express their love for God.

I have never been a person to judge anyone. Living a life in the church has been a blessing; it has opened many doors and long-lasting relationships. I have since grown to be a praise and worship leader at my home church and other churches and congregations. I currently hold a position at Good Shepherd Missionary Baptist Church as the music department president. I'm in charge of all the music for Sunday and afternoon services. It is my responsibility to make sure the music department is ready and on point to usher in the presence of the lord. I thank God for my gift every day for the ability to teach, sing, and read music.

Serving at a Baptist ministry has been different; it has kept me on my toes. Their services are timely and structured and in a certain order very consistent; we rarely deviate from the program. Overall being a (pk) pastor's kid has had its perks. The older I get; I realize that everybody has opinions on religion and who or what is your God. Religion- the belief in the worship of a superhuman controlling power, especially a personal God for gods. My belief in God is simple. At the end of the day, we all have to be held accountable for our actions and the choices that we make. He is the creator of the heavens and earth, and I believe him to be just who he is GOD.

CHAPTER 9 I'M NOT RELIGIOUS, I'M SPIRITUAL

> *"A true religion will have the humbleness to admit that only a few things are known, much more is unknown, and something will always remain unknowable. That 'something' is the target of the whole spiritual search. You cannot make it an object of knowledge, but you can experience it, you can drink of it, you can have the taste of it-it is existential."* Rajneesh

Once I decided to break from the opinions of organized religion, I searched for the phrase that would express my new state of being in terms of all things religious. And like so many in this new millennium, I embraced the axiom, "I'm not religious, I'm spiritual." What this phrase meant to me was that I didn't ascribe to any church, but I was still aware of God's existence and impact on my life. Everybody was saying it, and it sounded so hip, so now; in other words, WOKE. But even this new way to identify my belief system didn't quite satisfy my soul's longing for awareness of my actual state of being in the universe. For most of us who shared this new identity; it meant leaving one religion to embrace a new one like Buddhism or whatever the latest fad might be. Or at the very least, shedding the parts of our belief that no longer served us, but still holding fast to the elements we still liked like "love thy neighbor." That one still sounds good. But let's look at this construct of being "spiritual" for a moment.

While writing this book, I have been simultaneously filming the accompanying documentary recording the interviews with those souls who were kind enough to share their experiences with me and their points of view on the subject of religion. I find it strangely validating to hear so many participants refer to themselves as "spiritual, but not religious" or some form of this verbiage. There feels to me like there is some revival of mass awakening taking place in the world, allowing those who choose to be "woke" to begin to question the ideologies that they initially had force-fed to them and to demand some form of truth. And I noticed that no one that I asked could intelligently define what being "spiritual" really means. It's like being in some cryptic religious limbo of sorts. But still, somewhere within the search for truth lies the remnants of addiction to religion. We can't seem to let go completely. We're merely searching for a newer and better drug of choice to meet this need for religion without calling it the same. Deep down, we are in staunch denial of our addiction, just becoming fastidious about what drug we indulge in to meet our needs.

Spirituality

The term spiritual is defined as relating to, consisting of, or affecting the spirit (the immaterial intelligent or sentient part of a person). At face value, that definition could be viewed as ambiguous, so let's dig a little deeper. I looked at the synonyms for spiritual and unearthed the words bodiless, ethereal, formless, immaterial, incorporeal, insubstantial, nonmaterial, nonphysical, unbodied, and unsubstantial. Each of these points to the conclusion that spiritual things are those things that are invisible to the naked eye. Yet they exist within the realm of our reality. Love is a spiritual experience. Emotional pain is yet another spiritual experience, though you may not have thought to typically look at it that way. Emotions, thoughts, dreaming, or meditation are also spiritual expressions. As sentient beings, the totality of our consciousness and activity is spiritual if it does not involve the movement of our human body. So ironically, you are all spiritual anyway, whether you have the awareness of your spirituality or not.

For this book (and we can most certainly argue later if you feel so inclined), we will agree that human beings exist as threefold: body, mind (or consciousness), and spirit. The body is merely the earth suit in which we reside and navigate the realm of the earth and its atmosphere successfully. This suit sustains our existence, much like a space suit protects an astronaut in the dense atmosphere of space and provides a vehicle of mobility and utility for movement and perception of its surroundings. Its only other purpose is to procreate. Woefully, another addiction you might indulge in is in the preoccupation you have about your identification of self as it relates to your body. Are you pretty enough? Are you too fat? Am I tall enough? But we fail to understand the sole purpose of our earth suit for what it is and give too much credence to the design of its form than the universe would require for mere existence. The preoccupation with the body can divert the needed focus on the more important spiritual things. Does the question become who you are minus the pretty face or muscle-bound body? Who are you if you can no longer be the star athlete or become paralyzed and lose your limbs? You are who your spirit becomes as a result of the choices you make for yourself.

Stephen Hawking

Look at the great Stephen Hawking as some would regard his earth suit as almost useless. For his entire life, he suffered from the disease Amyotrophic lateral sclerosis (ALS), a progressive neurodegenerative disease that affects nerve cells in the brain and the spinal cord. Because of this disease, your motor neurons will die. As a result, the brain also loses the ability to control your muscles. In the end, the patient may become entirely immobile. Yet Hawking is considered to be one of the most prolific geniuses of our age with a keen mind and intelligence that surpassed even Albert Einstein's acclaim. Did his earth suit or body contribute or detract from his greatness? He and others like him validate that a hyper-focus on our external bodily form can potentially cause us to miss the real purpose of our being. What if Stephen Hawking were gifted with an athletic body with great strength, speed, and handsome looks to rival Brad Pitt? How likely do you think it would be that he would have traveled the same road? Is it far more likely that his attentions might have gone elsewhere? It's something to consider.

Beauty is in the Eye of the Beholder

Conversely, would Halle Berry have become as famous an actress if she were overweight and had terrible acne? One might argue that there are stars that have made it without the well-known brand of beauty, but do we laud them and their talent as the exception? Shouldn't the rule be that we judge people purely based upon their merit rather than their physical attributes? Would Honey Boo Boo have been such a novelty if she were not overweight? Would all of the "Little" people tv shows have a following if they were of average height? Beauty is an attribute whose intrinsic value is determined by society's definition of what features are most valuable, such as hair or eye color, body size and shape, or height. For example, according to Hitler, the pure race should have blond hair and blue eyes, which is ironic because he possessed neither of these traits. Historically, Hollywood fancied women who were blonde hair and blue-eyed as icons of beauty.

Harmony with the Universe and Others

Being spiritual is really about doing your soul work. Finding your connection to the universal mind is critical to establishing your soul's wellbeing. You can do this in many ways. It is sitting by the water and communing with the waves in the gentle breeze, basking in the crashing waves' rhythm. It is sitting on the mountain top and admiring the view. It is in the beauty of nature that displays its beauty so freely. It is sitting in communion with your soul and the universal subconscious in meditation and contemplating the possibilities of creation. It is fellowship with your fellow man nurturing a communion of love and tolerance. It is discovering your gifts and talents to share with the world beyond yourself. Your spirituality is your design for how you interact with the people in your life in times of peace, conflict, or sadness. It is your choice never to be offended. Your decision to never render evil for evil.

Your choice to see the best in the world and for those who you encounter. It is in the food you give to the poor and the comfort you offer the one who is weeping. Spirituality is your soul being, experiencing, and creating. Your spirituality is your soul's manifestation of God's presence and existence in this world for this time in space. Your spirituality is also present when you fail to do any or all of these things. So, you see, whether you like it or not, you are all spiritual.

The spirit is the spark of energy and the piece of the universe that resides within us all. It creates the existence of life. The dictionary describes it as the immaterial essence, animating principle, or actuating cause of an individual life. So, when we think about being "spiritual", what we mean is the system we employ to care for the wellbeing of the very essence of life within each of us. Spirituality is an awareness that you are a spirit that inhabits a human body. It is making a conscious effort to decipher which energies you allow to affect your soul. It is incumbent upon you to take great care of the spirit part of your being. You must feed it the proper nourishment. It is like the adage "you are what you eat." If you are around people who consistently bring negativity into your life, your spirit will be disturbed and unhappy. Likewise, if you feed your soul positive thoughts and good intentions towards the universe, you will know peace and serenity.

Next Steps and Takeaways from this chapter:

The Debate: Do you have to believe in God to be spiritual?

I have come to be very intentional about the energy that I allow to invade my space. As a spiritual being, I am susceptible to the effects of the energy of others. Have you ever been in a great mood, and when you got around a negative person, life is simply sucked out of the room? Conversely, have you ever been feeling down and decided to call that special someone that you know can always make you feel better, like maybe mom or a dear friend? Your spiritual life is all about your connection to the energy of the universe. Energy and time are not on a horizontal continuum, but a vertical line. The present, past, and future are all happening in the perpetual now. And all at the same time, there is both the positive and negative pole that exist within that continuum. Your spiritual health relies upon how well you balance yourself on the spectrum of positive and negative energy in your everyday life. If we fail to manage our spiritual health, we become reactive to the influences of whatever power is around us.

Take an assessment of the kinds of energy you allow in your space. Do you listen to that negative Nelly who whines and complains about everything? Do you often find yourself agreeing or even chiming in? Next time, try to turn that negative energy around with something positive and uplifting. Bring up the negative energy to a positive plane. If you find that person won't budge and is resistant to feeling better, then politely excuse yourself and take a moment to reflect. Do you harbor a misguided obligation to go to dinner or events with people that you know have a terrible attitude? You are only responsible for your serenity. No one has the right to infringe on your peace of mind. I don't care who they are.

I am not telling you to shut people out of your life, but you can set healthy boundaries with people who want to be in your life. You are not the garbage can for other people's negative energy. Faking the funk to be polite or "PC" in these situations places a strain and a drain on your spirit that you have the right to refuse. So if you know you have to go into a negative environment, like work for instance, you can raise your energy vibrations in such a way that will sustain you through unavoidable situations. And it is always your choice of how you respond to negative influences. And finally, use your voice. You can kindly and graciously set the tone for how you want negative people to engage with you. You might be surprised that they were unaware of their negative behavior. Or they may decide that they want to be offended, but that is a personal problem that they have to resolve with their God and with themselves.

Meet Miko in her own words:

I was brought up in the Baptist and Jehovah's Witness religions. Mom was Jehovah's witness. When I grew up, I began to explore other religions such as Buddhism, Judaism, Islam, and Hinduism. I was searching for truth, and I am still searching. Today, I am a believer in a Creator of all creations. I don't know if it's a she, or a he, or it; all I know is that there is a Creator. I'm a spiritual person, so I let the universe talk to me to learn its truth. Religion is taught. Spirituality is what you are born with-it's natural. It's like you know how when you put your hand in the fire, and it will burn you? In the same way, the Spirit will tell you right from wrong. You will get an eerie feeling.

The spirit is like the consciousness and subconscious. It will let you know when you are wrong and when you are doing right, but most of the time, you don't want to hear it. Spirituality is like good vs. evil. The good spirits are like a melody with a mellow voice. But the evil spirits, when they speak, sometimes they mumble. They speak in their language, and you get an eerie feeling. It's like you're spooked. You have to be careful not to allow evil spirits to open portals to other worlds and dimensions. There are dimensions to each planet that most people do not even know exist. So, I have trained myself to be still when my mind is racing. I can't hear or feel what the good spirits have to say unless I am calm. If I am always moving, I will listen to what the evil spirits are saying.

The brain is like an encyclopedia and keeps all of the memories. There is nothing that you can't remember. De Ja Vu comes from your subconscious mind to your conscious mind. And when you are operat-

ing on the plane of spirituality, you will become aware of things that no people can see, hear, feel, and even smell. It will blow your mind. You have to keep yourself surrounded in positive energy. And if you do not keep yourself fed with positive energy, people will keep you drained. If you are aware daily, you will see negativity before it gets to you. This is because negative spirits travel to and fro. Even though we are fleshly bodies, there are spirits roaming around us that are not in fleshly bodies.

In the past, I would walk away from people who wanted to tell me my future or a prophecy. I was afraid of whether or not they were real. But I would run into them again, and they would spook me. Somehow, we know one another. The way we know one another is how we encounter one another through spiritual connectivity. For this reason, you have to be grounded in positive energy in order to see what's going on around you truly.

When you pray, you have to trust and believe because nothing happens by mistake; it is all pre-ordained. Life is like an elevator. People get on with you, and when it stops, some people get on, and some get off. But once you get to your destination, there are only a few people there that will greet you and meet you. There are some people in your life that you cannot take to the next level. God will remove some folks, and you will let some go. My name is GRATEFUL. I am not from here. I'm passing through.

PART THREE: HOW WE RECOVER

Burning Desire
QUOTE OF THE DAY
DON'T STOP UNTIL YOU ARE FREE!

CHAPTER 10 THE LAW OF ATTRACTION

"Self-realization is, in fact, the only religion. For it is the true purpose of religion, no matter how people define their beliefs."
Paramahansa Yogananda

Everyone is so excited about the Law of Attraction these days. Typically, people are studying the Law of Attraction because they are looking for easy answers, getting rich quick, or earnestly desiring to change our lives. The good news is that the Law of Attraction is not a law that you have to "start doing" or "start using." The Law of Attraction is always working either for or against you despite your awareness of it. Simply put, the Law of Attraction says that like energy draws like energy unto itself. It works in conjunction with the Law of Vibration, which means that everything moves or vibrates; nothing rests. Everything you are experiencing and everything that is happening to you is something that you have attracted through thought.

The Law of Perpetual Transmutation tells us that energy is always moving into a physical form of creation. So, all creation begins through thought. I will give you a simple example of an invention through thinking. You are sitting around watching tv, and you see a commercial for an ice cream sundae. You remember that you have ice cream in your freezer. You don't have the caramel or the nuts. But the thought of a dessert is in your mind. So, you go to the store, purchase the nuts and caramel, come home, and voila, you have a caramel and peanut ice cream sundae. You just brought a thought into reality.

How it Works

The key to the law of attraction is the energy and emotion that is attached to the thought. Thoughts are energy, and the power that they create sends messages into the universe to attract similar energies unto itself. That upon which you expend thought energy will be drawn unto you whether you intended to attract it. The key to the ***successful*** application of the Law of Attraction is to be aware of its existence and the proper understanding of how it works. Are you familiar with the euphemism "birds of a feather flock together?" The flocking of the birds is another example of the law of attraction. Just as you are attracted to people who are like you, your thoughts draw other similar thoughts. If you think, "today is going to be a great day," the universe will bring experiences unto you that exemplify your idea of a great day. If you are thinking, "I know that they don't like me," the universe will bring unto you the experience that will allow them to demonstrate that they indeed do not like you. Even Paul wrote the following to the Philippians in the Bible:

> *Philippians 4:8 - Finally, brethren, whatsoever things are true, whatsoever things are honest, whatsoever things are just, whatsoever things are pure, whatsoever things are lovely, whatsoever things are of good report; if there be any virtue, and if there be any praise, think on these things.*

It is pure energy that propels the world, your thoughts, and all of existence into being. Fortunately, the management of your thoughts lies within your control to command. You have the potential to create your reality in the world as you desire it to be. This potential would suggest that you should be entirely intentional about what you think because those thoughts provide the source of energy necessary to spark and to give life to creation. The very reason that you exist in the physical world is to experience the world as God living as you. Your experiences allow God to know itself experientially. You must agree that none of us were born with a manual of instruction on how to live. You were not born with an inherent religious propensity. You were born with an instinctual drive to know yourself, create, and discover your purpose for being.

Thought and the Mind

The mind, also coined the "body-mind," is the consciousness that embodies our "thinking" actions and emotions. The fact is that you do not create thoughts. I challenge you to hear me out and then really "think" about it before you immediately reject its validity. I will admit that this concept was difficult for me to approbate at first glance. From the space of consciousness stems intelligence and creativity. Mindfulness allows us to access all of the universe's knowledge and, at the same time, wield the power of the universe to create.

Hence, all of the inventions of man, such as light bulbs, were always a possibility. Electricity has always been here on earth. Intelligence allows us to understand how to access, harness, and successfully utilize this resource. Television, the radio, and telephones are other phenomena that the intelligence we exemplify through invention allows us to enjoy. Historians have found versions of many of the utilities that we use today in earlier civilizations and various forms. Remember the adage, "there's nothing new under the sun?"

Thoughts arrive in us from the enormous database of the subconscious collective, wherever that is, and I humbly submit that I do not know or understand the complexities of the universal subconscious. No one can make such a claim. But I can speak from the experiences that I have had at various junctures in my lifetime. My experiences with ideas, dreams, and psychic energy validate the existence of such a realm. I have had dreams that came to pass. I used to prophesy with acute accuracy. I was able to see inside the universe from a meditative place and describe your house to you. This knowledge exists in the universe.

And I believe that under the right circumstances, anyone can tap into it. Thoughts simply come to us from the universe, and our conscious mind either accepts or rejects them.

Consider this, have you ever thought to answer a question, but someone else spoke up, and you thought, "That's what I was going to say." Or seen an invention on television and thought, "They stole my idea!" These incidents occur because thoughts appear to us from the "somewhere" and are not necessarily exclusive. Remember, we are all connected to the universal consciousness (more on that later.) But the point is, when a thought or idea comes to you, your consciousness can filter that thought and decide whether to ponder it or reject it. The lack of awareness of the origin of thought has fooled us into believing that ideas come from us, and therefore we must act upon them.

Since we were not born with instructions, we were born with the ability to learn. Words do not teach; we learn from our experiences. Through our experiences and our intuition's unction, we discover the laws of the universe and the effects these laws have on the outcome of our choices. The thought is the most powerful tool and resource ever given to man. From thought, you provide the Law of Attraction its purpose—to bring to you what you want. You see, the whole world is the Garden of Eden, our paradise to enjoy. God was pretty cool to provide the Law of Attraction, which never fails, for it ensures that we enjoy our deepest desires. The problem is that we have corrupted our experience with the Law of Attraction by both misunderstanding its existence and ignorance of its existence. If you think about it, it all makes sense. Einstein and science taught us that there is nothing new under the sun. Even the Bible tells us so.

"Creation only occurs in the mind. Everything that comes from that process of thought materializes in the physical world from materials that already exist." K. D. Foy

How it Can Work Against Us

Religion has conditioned us to forego our ability to take responsibility for the creation of the outcome of our lives. Whether it be obtaining some level of enlightenment or achievement, or following some prescribed set of laws. We learn to rely on the goodwill of some God or the other. If life is going well, then you are blessed, and conversely, if things are going wrong, you must somehow be cursed or guilty of receiving a god's displeasure. You do not learn that you are God, and as such, your destiny lies in your own hands to manage. It is as though we are the store owners, but we have given someone we don't know, have never seen, or never even spoken to the authority to dictate how our business runs. Then we are surprised when we go bankrupt or feel "blessed" when things go the way we intended. You have given the responsibility to an entity that has already given you the power to manage yourself. Remember, the Law of Attraction works whether you are aware of it or not.

Now think back to a situation that did not work out for you. How did you feel about it? Think about a recent disappointment. If you examine your thought process and your attitude toward the situation, you can typically discern how your thoughts and subsequent actions influenced your outcome. Ideas are the energy that sparks the creation of all things. So even if you concentrate on hoping things do not go wrong, things will most likely go wrong because the "wrong" is what you are giving energy to through thought. One should, instead, focus on what you do want to see happen instead. Have you ever tried to do your level best to get over a breakup with a loved one only for them to call you out of the blue suddenly? I know I have.

If you give energy to the thought that has always been, you will continue to get the same results. For example, have you ever uttered the phrase, "I can't help it, that's just the way I am"? Or, "that's how I was brought up to do it." Even though you may consciously desire things to be different, if your inner belief is rooted in how things have always been, you will still get the same results. It's the definition of insanity, right? If you are single and do not want to be, your focus should be on the fact that you can't seem to find anyone but instead on what you hope to see. You should not get bogged down by focusing on how lonely you are. Or how everyone else has someone, why not me? By focusing on thoughts of loneliness, you are attracting similar feelings towards yourself within the universe. And consequently, the result in the physical world will be you—alone. I know I quote the Bible quite a bit, but the Bible has a lot of wisdom that you can benefit from consuming. So here is another one, Proverbs 18:24 A man that hath friends must shew himself friendly: and there is a friend that sticketh closer than a brother. In other words, "Be the change you want to see in the world."

Awareness vs. The Mind

When you decide to capitalize on the benefits of proactively employing the law of attraction to your life, your most significant obstacle will lie in how well you manage your awareness and your mind, respectively. You have to understand that the two are entirely separate entities. You may have never thought about it this way before, but we will do a simple test to prove that awareness and the mind are quite distinct. What we will discover is that we are controlled by what stimulus has the attention of our awareness. ***That which governs your awareness governs your reality.***

I would like to demonstrate this for you so that it will be a reader participation activity here. So, think about the room you are sitting in right now. Are you seated or standing? What is the temperature like in the room? Is it comfortable? Is it hot, or is it cold? What kind of sounds do you hear right now? Is it loud and noisy? Can you listen to cars? Now, think about the last party you were invited to attend. Was it personal, or was it work-related? Were there a lot of people there? How was the food? Were there drinks? Were they free? Did you have a good time? Now, think about the first time you had a close relative to pass away. Was it someone you loved? Was the funeral somber? Were there a lot of people in attendance? Did you cry? Now, bring your attention back to the room you are in right now. Is it still quiet, or are there more noises? Are you still comfortable?

Dandapani, an Ex-monk now entrepreneur, explained it this way: "Life is a manifestation of where you invest your energy." Awareness is like a ball of light. The mind is like a room that stores all of your thoughts and emotions. And according to Dandapani, "Where awareness goes, energy flows." And with questions I asked above, I was able to move your awareness from memory to memory. Your awareness navigated you from place to place like rooms in a house. Your energy flowed to the room that your awareness flowed to access each memory. It is really that simple to see the difference in awareness and consciousness.

I am currently working with a young woman in recovery, and she has mentioned to me several times that she is scatter-brained, and her mind is all over the place. The more accurate statement would be that her "awareness" is going all over the place. You will want to master the skill of controlling your awareness if you're going to take control of where you give energy to thought and begin to control what you attract with those same thoughts. I describe this phenomenon as what I like to call the "Jerry Springer Effect." You remember the show that you loved to hate. The one with all of those crazy people sprung forth from an unlimited pool of pain and degradation. Some genius at the show figured out how to train us all—the crowd and the guests—like Pavlov's dog. Whenever the guest and their protagonist get into a heated argument over who stole whose boyfriend, or what boyfriend was cheating with which best friend's girl, the show did a little thing to jump things off. Do you remember what it was? Well, I will remind you—DING DING DING DING DING!!! And whenever that bell goes off, what do the guests immediately start to do—FIGHT! And what do we, as the audience, expect to see—A fight! And do they deliver? I can only answer with a resounding YES! We all have Jerry Springer bells in our lives that once they are rung, we respond with all of the vigor of a dog with a juicy bone. You react without thought and after a while, without rhyme or reason. These "triggers," as we now affectionately call them these days, are deeply embedded within our subconscious and impact how we unwittingly respond to the stimulus of life.

For me, my sure-fire, never fail, don't even TRY me Jerry Springer bell was calling me a bitch. If you called me a bitch, I didn't care who you were or where we were. I was going to proceed to knock your block off! In my twisted sense of self-esteem, I thought that if someone disrespected me by calling me the "b" word, it was my absolute duty to my soul to fight you. How retarded is that logic? Yet, you all have those bells to which you all respond that drive your awareness of what is best for you or what you hope to accomplish in life to some broken place of unhealed woundedness. These reactions will cause you to be your own worst enemy by giving all of your power away.

You save your soul by finding the awareness of these triggers, and with that awareness, you can systematically deactivate them. You replace those "triggers" with a new thought, empowering thought that creates the life you want to see manifest for you daily. You choose NOT to be offended by veiled attacks against your character that you know not to be true. You decide NOT to get "pissed off" at the car that cut you off. You choose NOT to react to someone being unkind, and not only that, you now decide if you even want to dignify these triggers with a response. With awareness comes power. And you do not need any religion to realize your awareness and manifest your best sense of self-purpose.

"When you change the way you look at things, the things you look at change." Wayne Dyer

Cause and Effect

We have already discussed the idea of thought being energy.

Creation is thought over time, made manifest in the physical world. You can also examine the uni versal law of the Law of Cause and Effect. Both cause and effect are mostly the same as the outcome is what becomes of the cause when it becomes real. In other words, the result is the manifestation of cause. Einstein stated it this way that "every action has an equal and opposite reaction." I like to simply say, "You may get by, but you won't get away!" Or who hasn't mentioned the old goody "what goes around, comes around." The Bible says it this way: "You reap what you sow."

There are many benefits to understanding universal laws. If there is a God who has placed certain sanctions on our human behavior, those sanctions are made known to us from experiencing the impact of "breaking" these universal laws. Lack of awareness of universal law does not exempt you from their influence, much like in human law. Ignorance of the law does not exempt you from guilt when breaking human law.

By taking a closer look at what may be the cause of some of the manifestations in your life, you can understand why you received the accompanying effect of that cause. If you are thinking negative thoughts, the result would be negative results. Let me give you an example. I wanted a raise in my old job because they did not pay me what I thought I was worth. I complained for years to no avail. Why pay me more when they are getting what they want from me now? So, I made a decision. I would go and get a certification that my company valued. I paid the $4,000 for the course out of my own money because I could not get the company to pay for it.

After I received the certification, I updated my resume and applied for a new position, interviewed, and got hired for the job. The effect I received was a $25,000 a year bump in my pay that sent me over six figures. What is the message here? They did not pay me more because I did not have more to offer. When I got my certification, I became more valuable and thus received the rate of pay I felt worthy of receiving. The fact is that if you cannot get to the root cause of your experiencing what you experience, you are unable to change the effect on your life.

Raising Your Vibration

Whether you know it or not, you have an energy field created by the energy vibrations that radiate from your being. This energy is vibrating at different frequencies. Putting it all together, we already stated that like attracts like. So, it is with energy vibrations. Have you ever gone into a room and could feel that the tension in the air was thick? Have you ever been having a great time with friends, and then someone unwelcome or uninvited intruded upon your space, and the energy drop was almost tangible? And who is brave enough to admit that they have met someone for the first time and some reason, you "just don't like them'?

It is vital to have an awareness of where you are vibrating at any given time. Sickness, anger, negativity, happiness, and everything in the universe vibrates at a specific frequency. Higher frequencies house your positive energies, and lower frequencies house your negative energies. As a result, high energies do not attract low energies. For example, if you are in a fantastic mood, happy, and floating on top of the world when you encounter a depressed, sad friend, the two of you will not be able to engage. One of you would have to either rise to the higher frequency or descend to the lower frequency of the other. If equilibrium is not possible, you will both likely part ways or end the interaction. There will exist a mutual discomfort if you each try to maintain your vibrations in the same place at the same time.

The attraction of your energy frequency in thought has a similar effect on the universal subconscious mind. If you think negative thoughts like "I know they don't like me," you will unwittingly attract the same feelings from the universe. Suddenly you might think, "See how they are looking at me?" Or "I know they are talking about me." Your aim should be to think about the things that you desire to draw unto yourself. "I am friendly, so other people like me." Or, "I will make friends today and meet fascinating people." This energy will solicit like energies in the room and draw others who have similar thoughts to you.

Have you ever wondered why certain people like to flock together in an environment where you have to pick teams or play a game? It is because they are vibrating at similar energy vibrations. It is the same thing that occurs between lovers who attract each other because of the vibrations they are sending. You know, you spot each other from across a room. You are drawn to each other by the connection of your energies. When they come near you, your heart races, and your stomach leaps in anticipation. We call it chemistry, but it is indeed, energy.

One of the most important things that I want to mention about the importance of awareness about your energy vibrations is to examine the links between your consciousness and the undesirable occurrences in your life. For instance, you may ask yourself why you tend to attract potential mates who always cheat? Or why do people always seem to avoid you in social settings? Why are you still picked on or abused by others? There is something inside of you that is sending out a vibration to attract the undesired behavior. Once identified, you can then change your thought and raise your frequency in that area to change the dynamics of that particular action. Your thought energy should move toward higher ideas of your self-worth and value that suggest that you are deserving of love, respect, and kindness. Have you ever heard that no one likes someone desperate for love? Have you ever been that way and repelled potential suitors who would not even give you a chance? You may be sending a vibration that suggests that you are unlovable, lonely, and desperate, and such a negative vibration recoils the other person. In this way, opposites do not attract, after all.

It is in your express best interest to guard yourself and the energy that you allow in your space. You have the supreme right to be intentional, selfish, and self-seeking in this regard. Remember, what happens to you is a direct result of what you allow.

If you passively allow people to mistreat, misuse, or disregard you negatively, you allow space for the negative consequences of that low-frequency energy that you absorb. That negativity presents within you in the form of resentments, anger, low self-esteem, feelings of worthlessness, anxiety, depression, and again, I could go on and on. It is unnecessary to fabricate that you don't care, justify another's actions with statements such as "they didn't mean it" or "that's just how they are." You do not have to allow negative energy in your space. If you are unable to raise the energy level to something higher with kindness and love, you should allow yourself to remove yourself from the environment.

Next Steps and Takeaways from this chapter:

The Debate: Is your life path constructed for you by stochastic randomness or a deterministic model preordained by God?

Reflect on what you have been attracting in your life. Take a look at everything you have going on in your life: your career, your relationship, your possessions, your love life, your children. Everything you see is a result of what you have attracted to yourself through thought and the Law of Attraction. Do you know what you want to see? What things would you like to change? Think about the root cause of why you have attracted things into your life that you don't necessarily want. Have you settled for some ideas? Have you made decisions just to please others? Are you working a job only to pay the bills? Are you living in fear that is keeping you from living your best life?

Consider how much responsibility you take for the choices you make in your own life. Do you permit yourself to dream big in some parts of your life but not in others? For example, do you rock in your job, but sell yourself short in the love department? Do you trust your instincts when it comes to advising others, but do not apply the same amount of confidence in your talents and abilities? My advice is to become your own number one fan and trust your inner guidance to attract that which will support your best life.

Meet Hannah in her own words:

I grew up in the Jewish tradition which means that we live by the Torah. It has a total of 613 commandments that are also included the Bible. These commandments serve as guidelines for how we should live and treat each other. We observe many Jewish holidays. Shabbat is the Sabbath which we observed from sundown on Friday until sundown on Saturday. Other familiar holidays are Rosh Hashanah, the Jewish new year, Yom Kippur, and Hannukah.

One familiar tradition about Jewish people is our kosher diet. This means we do not eat meat that has not been prepared in our traditional way. As a kid, I used to wonder why we couldn't eat at regular fast food restaurants, but my parents explained that we only eat kosher so I learned not to question it anymore. It became a part of who we were. We used to joke about it after a while that "those people are eating bad meat." But it was all in fun.

The biggest difference that I noticed with my friends who were not Jewish is that they did not observe the Sabbath every week like we did. My family was strict so we couldn't go out and do fun things with our friends during the Sabbath like hanging out or watching tv. We didn't get to go to the movies or work or anything. I really respected these times with my family though because we would do many things together. We would go to the synagogue for prayers, prepare our meals in a special way, and really get to bond. Until this day, I haven't gone out on a Friday or Saturday with my friends. The Sabbath is really important to us.

Even though our faith is very important to me, it did create a dilemma for me at school because I couldn't participate in the extracurricular activities that fell on the weekends. No sporting events or school plays for me which was kind of sad but I understood. But my friends weren't always so understanding. They thought it was really unfair that I had to give up so much for my religion. But for me, it was a choice and not a chore.

CHAPTER 11 YOU ARE "I AM"-BE WATER

> *"Knowledge of one's identity, one's self, community, nation, religion, and God, is the true meaning of resurrection, while ignorance of it signifies hell." Elijah Muhammad*

Another misconception in monotheistic or henotheistic religions is the intimation of separation from God. In most religions, God is some being or force that is greater than ourselves. To be clear, the totality of the universe is more significant than any single one of us. But each of us is a part of the collective that is God. You are not detached and removed from the totality of God. Furthermore, we are all part of each other. You do not have to search or seek out God. You are the part of God that chose to live in your mortal body for this time. Because the entirety of God could not know himself as one being. Remember what you learned about relativity. God could not know itself as God without anything to relate itself too. She had to create parts of herself in the form of creation. This creation allows God to recognize itself experientially through each one of us. Think of it this way, if you were the only person in the world, there would be no way that you could know yourself because there would be no one to compare yourself to for you would be alone. The creation story in the bible and the Koran suggests that God was lonely and said to itself, "Let us make a man." It is primarily from this place of "everythingness" and "nothingness" that God created everything from Himself.

We also talked about the personification of God and the human emotions that we project upon the supreme being. Gods that men have designed are to either be prayed to, worshipped, or sought for judgment. These gods are either invisible, created by man, or recruited in nature. We give natural anomalies such as natural disasters or illness supernatural origins to explain their existence. But let's take a look at one element found in nature: one of the most powerful—water. Think about the ocean. It comes to know itself as rivers, oceans, lakes, ponds, creeks, springs, snow, ice, rain, etc. It is all water, right? They are examples of the many manifestations of water having the same chemical makeup—H2O.

And so, it is with humanity and God. We are all manifestations of "I AM"—water. Water is the softest sub stance on earth. But given time, water can carve mountains into caverns. Water always takes the path of least resistance. It never fights for its way. It will directly go around the obstacles and forge a path where no path existed. Water creates its own path regardless of how impossible the road may appear to be. It is in harmony with nature and the universe. Its power can be felt for miles. Its brute force can destroy cities. Yet we all need it to live. It composes 70% of our bodies and is in the composition of nearly everything on earth. It is worth more than gold if you cannot easily possess it. Earth would be an inhabitable planet without it.

The great Bruce Lee said, "Water can flow, or it can crash. Be water, my friend." Water assumes the form of whatever vessels contain it. Water is fluid and relentless in its pursuits. And just as water is a part of every living thing, so it is that God is in everything. And the piece of God that resides in us embodies us with the power, resolution, and strength that the whole of God possesses. We each have the power of creation surging loudly within us, craving to fulfill its purpose. All of the universe's energy is divided into everything that we see, touch, hear, and experience. In my layman's mind, the power of the universe is like a cake, and each part of creation, both animate and inanimate, are incremental slices of that cake. Therefore, we are all connected. But more exceptional minds than my own have made scientific discoveries that validate my simple idea of the cake.

The scientific Law of Conservation of Masses proposed by Antoine Lavoisier in 1785, states that matter is neither created nor destroyed. Later in 1842, Julius Robert Mayer discovered the Law of Conservation of Energy, which states that energy is neither created nor destroyed. Both of these theories were consolidated in 1907 by Albert Einstein. He announced his discovery of the Law of Conservation of Mass-Energy (E=mc2), and, as a consequence, the total amount of mass and energy in the universe is constant. The bible has a scripture which predates all of these theories in where the wise Solomon shared his philosophy:

"The thing that hath been, it is that which shall be; and that which is done is that which shall be done; and there is no new thing under the sun." Ecclesiastes 1:9

It stands to reason that if there is nothing new that is being created or destroyed, today's existence connects to that which shall exist tomorrow and equal to that which existed on yesterday. Which begs the question, is it true that someone is born every time someone dies? What is the source of the pool of energy that creates the body-mind and the soul? Is it merely recycled energy? Many people claim to remember previous lives. I used to think these people were nuts! But is it possible or even plausible that they are experiencing memories of the person who previously possessed the piece of energy that animates their life force? Is there residual memory and lingering impressions that travel from person to person?

"True religion is real living; living with all one's soul, with all one's goodness and righteousness." Albert Einstein

When you understand your oneness with God, you know your harmony with self. You can take ownership of how you respond and whether you respond to every experience you encounter. There are no victims, only volunteers. What if you decided to identify with "I" solely? And what is "I" or "I AM"? "I AM" is the first name that you come to know. Hello there, and who are you? You, "I am _____." "I am" is how you communicate your state of being, wellness, or discomfort. I am hungry, or I am upset. "I am" is the universal name for everyone that exists no matter the culture, race, or creed. "I am" encompasses every fiber of every being, yet you live in a state of denial of "I am." You forego your power to others. For example, "she didn't love me." "They have it in for me." How about this one, "If it's God's will." It is called the blame game in laymen's terms. You empower "he," "she," and "they" to define your worth, your value, and your self-esteem. First of all, who the hell are "they"? Why should "they" matter so much when you take an assessment of your life and its instrumental value to the rest of the world?

According to Abraham Hicks, there are only two emotions: What feels right and what feels wrong. These two feelings are your internal barometer to let you know how your soul feels about whatever you are doing. This intuition is your "I." Your soul is the part of God that exists within you to give you animation and life. It is this lifeforce that, when gone, causes you to die physically. The body can sometimes function for a short time without your lifeforce. The body can even continue to live with the aid of life support technology. But when the soul or the lifeforce is gone, the body will eventually die because the "God" part of you is gone. You become like water once evaporated. You return to the source.

Some have surmised that your purpose as a human being and reason for being is to serve others. This idea is a fallacy of sorts. Your goal can be to help others if and only if your "I" has made that decision for itself. Let me explain. Each soul has a plan for what it wishes to accomplish in this physical world. Let me put it this way if you were asked the question, "If money were no object, what would you want to do with your life?" The response would most likely be your soul's desire for purpose—"I am" a writer, or singer, or whatever. This thing would make you feel good inside.

For example, you may feel fulfilled and gratified when volunteering at the soup kitchen on the weekends. But you don't dedicate yourself to volunteering because it doesn't pay the bills. Your "I" wants to serve the less fortunate, and until you can verbalize the statement "I want to serve others," you will most likely feel discontentment about what you choose to do as a job or career. Your work is to understand what your soul longs to do. Once discovered, whatever it is that you desire to "be" as "I Am" can provide you a living and fulfillment. You may have to exercise your creator muscles to uncover the way to accomplish it, but it is certainly possible. Be water and flow until you create the path to your soul's desire.

If Necessary, Hurt Then Heal Yourself

If you have not served your "I am" well and settled for whatever has come your way, you may find yourself deeply frustrated. Now I am most assuredly confident that the idea of "hurting then healing" yourself might sound unequivocally absurd to some of you. But you might find that this process may well be the most powerful tool of empowerment that you have in your arsenal for navigating your life. Too often, you may have given away your power to another, leaving yourself vulnerable to their interpretation of who you are. Since you are the only one who gets to define your value, your worth, and your journey, do not allow someone else to hurt you and hold you spiritually hostage to their devaluation of your idea of "Who I Am."

So, what do I mean when I say this? I am glad you asked. I am on marriage number three. If you asked me what happened to my first two marriages in the past, I conceivably would have responded with a monologue of infractions my exes committed against me. But the reality is that I chose all three of them—for better or for worse. The only way I was able to remove myself from the difficulties I encountered in my previous marriages was to hurt myself then heal. I had to accept that I had made the wrong decision in choosing my mates. It didn't matter why I did it. They didn't do anything to me. I chose poorly, and therefore I reaped the negative consequences. But guess what? Since I made the unfortunate decision, I alone was able to rectify the situation and allow myself the opportunity to heal.

"Healing is only done from the inside out." K. D. Foy

You will never get your healing for any wound from outside of yourself. If you take medicine, your body ingests it. If you scrape your knee, regenerative cells are formed by the cells within your body. Likewise, if you are hurt within your heart or soul, you cannot be healed by things outside of yourself. The good news is that you have all of the power you need inside you to recover. Albeit guidance from a trusted guide, leader, or even professional may serve you to help to identify the root cause of your pain and provide suggestions for recovery. But ultimately, the healing is done by you from within yourself.

If you have toxic people, a negative work environment, and an uncomfortable religious situation, you can assume responsibility for your choices and change your setting. It makes no sense to prolong your suffering with the following justifications:

1. I am just trying to make it work.

2. Nobody's perfect.

3. You have to deal with something, no matter where you go.

Your serenity and your peace of mind is your responsibility. The results that come from staying in unhealthy environments as a sacrifice for others only lead to adverse outcomes. Rarely will others recognize your gift and reward you kindly and sing your praises. Even the bible tells us that a prophet is without honor in his own house in Luke 4:16.

There are many situations that you don't need to "pray" about for answers. A blind person can see that you are in a position that is unhealthy for you. God does not care or benefit from your suffering. I get it that this concept may be difficult to hear. But as I will say several times throughout this book, your purpose here on earth is to have the best experience that you can imagine. You are not doing God any favors by being treated poorly by others. If God loves you, then why would He want to see you suffer? Does he want to teach you a lesson? Really? I don't think so. God gave us the ability to intellectually assess a situation and make the best decision for ourselves to see the best outcome. Our emotions are internal tools that make you aware of how a case is affecting us from within your soul. If you make an error, then just acknowledge it, hurt yourself if necessary, and remove yourself from that circumstance—then heal.

Water doesn't fight the status quo; it creates a new path to forge forward. You will never see water flow upward or against the current, and neither should you. So many of our problems come from trying to control others within a situation of our creation. You tell yourself things like, "If only he would..." Or "Things would perfect if they would only change this or stop that...." Then we pray to God for "them" to change. Sound familiar?

Next Steps and Takeaways from this chapter:

The Debate: Where do you draw the line between taking advice from others and making your own choices?

I challenge you to consider the debate question. Assess your life and look for ways that you settle or live your life in a certain way because you are trying to please others. Are you working the job that you can't wait to get up every morning to get to it? Do you want to do standup comedy or open that cupcake business? Do you love working with animals? Do you hate going to church, but you are in religion you don't accept to keep a loved one in your life? When an addict is in active addiction, they often do many things that they would not ordinarily do if not under the influence. Things like stealing from loved ones, abandoning their children, selling their bodies, or performing acts that they inwardly find abominable. So, what are you doing right now in your life that you honestly hate to impress someone or please someone else?

Everything that you need to exist in the world and to know God is inside you. The means for understanding the creator are inside of you at birth. Intuition is the universe's internal guidance and navigation system to lead you through life's expedition. Just like the animals instinctively and intuitively know their place in the world, so do we. But our natural connection to God and the infinite energy is suffocated by our learning of man's laws of conduct. Look at indigenous, so-called uncivilized, people, and how they harmonize with nature and the world taking only what they need. They show respect to mother earth, and mother earth provides her bounty.

"There is no greater gift you can give or receive than to honor your calling. It's why you were born. And how you become most truly alive." ~ Oprah Winfrey

In assuming the responsibility for your life's journey, you have to periodically take stock of your actions to see how your soul is being affected. It is very easy to become numb to the mundane day-to-day functionality of your existence. You die a little bit each day you fail to accomplish your soul's calling. It is a calling because your spirit is calling out to you to say, "I don't like this." Or "I am not happy here." Yet you choose to ignore your inner "I am" at the expense of your happiness. Is that fair? The soap opera says you only have one life to live. Arguably, that may or may not be valid. But whether you have lived before or get to live again in another lifetime, you don't get to take your memories with you. It would behoove you to maximize this life's possibilities to the fullest fully. It is not a question of time because you always live in the infinite now. But how are you feeling right now? If it is not happiness and peace, you are doing yourself a disservice.

Meet Rashim in his own words:

As a teenager, I was a religious fanatic you could say. But by the time I hit high school and eventually went to college, I started to drift away from religion. It was more about hanging out with my friends than praying and going to the mosque. Like most people, I have gone through multiple changes about my spirituality depending on what was going on in my life at the time. But I guess it's probably like that for most people.

My spirituality sort went up and down through the years. In my religion, you are required to pray five times a day. This is pretty hard to do when you have a hectic schedule, but I do my best to pray as many times as I can. But in my opinion, true spirituality is not so much about all of the rituals of my religion and more about my personal relationship with Allah. So for me, it's more about the core principles and values of Islam more than anything. I try to be a good person and follow the basic traditions of Islam as way of daily living.

I have reached a point in my life where I am trying to find my own way. Life isn't black and white, so you have to make your own decisions about how you want to live your life. Like I may want to have a drink with friends from time to time. Or I may get deeply involved with a girl and we are not married. But overall, I know that though all of my decisions are not the best. I try to learn from my mistakes and do better the next time.

I try to keep up with as many of the Islamic traditions and holidays as I can. I also have certain traditions that are a part of my life like Ramadan. Ramadan is where we fast for thirty days. And even though I don't always get them in, I try to pray as close to five times a day as I can. Praying is like eating, it's food for the soul. And when I pray, I use the headscarf as a show of respect. I also enjoy meditation and reflection. My religion gives me a balance and helps to keep me from doing things that I might regret later.

CHAPTER 12 SEX, LGBTQ, AND RELIGION

> *"I'll tell you this: Religion is far more of a choice than homosexuality. And the protections that we have, for religion—we protect religion—and talk about a lifestyle choice! That is absolutely a choice. Gay people don't choose to be gay. At what age did you choose not to be gay?" Jon Stewart*

Most religions address sexuality in some way in their holy texts. They offer guidelines that provide a basic expectation for sexual conduct. Typically, religions speak to the hope of a marital bond in various forms. The relationship may be monogamous or polyamorous (consists of one man and one or more women that enter the contract of marriage). The Bible considers adultery, infidelity in the union as sin. Fornication, which is sex before marriage, is also frowned upon in both Judeo-Christian and Islamic faiths. Over time, views have changed and broadened in scope to include provisions for alternative lifestyles. But historically, there is much debate about what sexual acts are appropriate and with whom they are relevant. More puritanical sects view the sexual act as only suitable for procreation, and they see pleasurable sexual acts as sin.

There has been much derision and debate over homosexuality throughout religion and throughout history. So, it depends on what point of history you lived as to whether or not homosexuality was considered a sin or as normal behavior. The Bible suggests that it is morally wrong for a man to lie with a man as he would a woman in Leviticus 18:22. We debate the question of whether or not you are born gay or if it is a choice. Is it a sin or not? Is being gay natural or unnatural? And what of bisexuality? It gets complicated there.

But be at ease, I do not intend to validate or invalidate the practice of same-sex love. Nor do I have the right to do so. The choice is your own to make. The fact is God could care less about who you sleep with or choose to love. No more than he counts every lie that you tell or piece of candy a kid may steal. Love is love. And the possibility that homosexuality will somehow create a reduction in the human population is no more likely than unmarried people will stop having unprotected sex, producing children out of wedlock. Or even less likely, get women, or men for that matter, to quit the oldest profession in the world.

But let's examine the topic of sexuality a bit because it is imperative to understand the practice of being gay related to religious ideology. Despite the perceived progress, there is still much persecution, shaming, and abuse of those considered gay. Because homosexuality has to do with sex, a subject of immense sensitivity, some religious leaders have named themselves judge, jury, and in some cases, executioner (of your character or reputation) for those found guilty of committing the carnal sin of homosexuality. It amazes me how much of religion entreats its followers to deny one's natural desires.

How We View Sexuality

Before we can even consider the issue of homosexuality, let us take a peek at our history with sexuality. Many of our sex views are reliant upon which part of the world you live or the time in history. The greatest misconception surrounding sex that has its roots in religion is that the act of sexual intercourse is designed merely to perpetuate life in the form of procreation.

The belief is that intercourse is only pleasant to motivate humans to perform the act. But if this were so, every act of sex would create life, and you would probably only have the desire to copulate when pregnancy is most likely. Look at the animal kingdom and how the animals respond to potential mates when they are in heat. The truth is that God made sex to be one of the highest forms of human intimacy possible. A sexual act is the most intimate act that you can engage in with another human being. In my opinion, the only moral expectations for sex should be to give and show love to another human being capable of receiving and returning that love in a meaningful way.

American society has perpetuated a sense of dirtiness, shame, and ugliness around the idea of human sexuality because of its pseudo-religious history. From a very young age, you are encouraged to hide your body and the feelings that naturally occur within your body. If a young child sexually touches him or herself, this natural curiosity is squashed and immediately scolded as inappropriate and wrong. You tell your sons that if they masturbate, they will go blind for Christ's sake. You hide your nakedness from your children and create a sense of shame that, for many, creates much sexual confusion and even aberrations in sexual conduct later in life.

The shame is embedded so deeply into my psyche that all of the learning in the world cannot remove it. I can recall when I was on my tour of Europe at the age of sixteen, that one of my friends was traveling with his family. I went into their hotel room, and his mom walked through the room stark naked in front of all of us. I thought this was the most brazen thing I had ever seen. But their family was carefree with their bodies and had no shame about being naked. It is a shame that your mind can immediately go to a dark place about a thing while others can live freely with the same scenario.

Your fear of sexuality has given way to all of the sexual perversion and sexual deviance that grows from the dark places of shame that you, in turn, instill into your children. Sex is a natural part of all of us, yet we have given so much power to this natural action that it cannot merely be what it is in its simplicity- the physical expression of love between human beings. If you learn to appreciate sex for what it is rather than demonize sex for all of the horrible things that it can be, you would not have all of the problems that you inadvertently create. Human attraction is a natural reaction of one person's energy to another's, as we mentioned earlier in the chapter on the Law of Attraction that like attracts like.

In some cultures, they celebrate sexuality. In these societies, there is little if any sexual misconduct such as rape. On the small island of Mangaia in the Cook Islands, sexuality is taught to their children as early as toddler age. They are a sexually free society that looks at sexual prowess as an asset. Children are trained by their elders from an early age to masturbate, appreciate the opposite sex's body, and please their partner sexually. They pair young boys with older women to hone their sexual ability as proficient lovers. I encourage you to research them further if you find this standpoint interesting. It is here in America that we still foster a hypocritical aura of puritanical piety. Because of how we hide our sexuality, we like to give the impression of being a sexually moral country. However, there is a steaming undercurrent of sexual proclivity that ravishes our nation's underbelly.

Self-Hatred

Many members of the LGBTQ community who grow up in religious homes hear that they are wrong, abominations, and evil. Sadly, there are those parents who send their children to programs designed to "change" their children into "straight" individuals. There are groups like Exodus International that was founded to "help people who wished to limit their homosexual desires." This group teaches its youth to deny their natural impulses and cleave to a sexual identity that belongs to the church and to denounce their desires. They learn that God will not accept them the way that they are. It sends a mixed message when you say that God is love, but this same God hates any of His creation.

I have yet to hear a reason that makes any sense to me as to why God would care who you loved or had sex within any situation? Why would a creator of the world have an opinion about every sexual encounter with its people? When you frame the question, that way, it sounds bizarre. But yet, She must care somehow, and despite His loving nature, we have decided that It chooses to hate the "happy" people in the world. But yet, He made homosexuality a possibility in the universe. It would seem that if They were categorically against homosexuality, there would be no way for homosexuality to occur in nature. Was He not powerful enough to prevent the behavior? Or is it just another forbidden fruit placed within the garden of love to tempt some of us and to fail as human beings like Adam and Eve did in the garden?

There is so much hatred in the world. Race against race, color against color. But hatred of self is the most damaging form of hatred that exists. You cannot love anyone else if you do not love yourself. Any religion you embrace should foster a love of self at its core because anything less is an insult to whatever God you serve. You must make enough choices, such as what career is the right one, how much education you should get, and how to survive against all of the competition to succeed in life. Your religion should be the safest place for self-expression, growth, and well-being if you choose to follow one.

If your religion does not accept you for who you are, then you might want to consider why you choose to participate in that faith. I would also question trying to reform your religion into accepting a lifestyle that it preaches against, for that is a form of deception that is inauthentic. And again, if there are exceptions to the rule, the rule is null and void. It is as if to say, "Okay, we know we said that homosexuality is wrong, but we now changed our minds. You guys are okay." Religion should not be a club where they change the rules to who can or cannot join.

The Hypocrisy of Religious People

One of the things that I find disturbing about organized religion is the fulsomeness that I see in many groups. While many religions speak of sin as acts that are against God's law, some sins seem to be categorically "worse" than others. If sin creates separation from God, you might as well do whatever you want if you are going to commit any. Those who are of religious beliefs have historically persecuted those considered to be gay in their sexual orientation to an extreme that far exceeds their disdain for other so-called sins. Those parishioners who commit the sins of lust, fornication, theft, or adultery or any number of religious infractions are forgiven or not even addressed by the collective. This hypocrisy breeds resentment among those who are gay and perpetuates the need to hide or assimilate to feel the same acceptance as the other members of the group.

The other side of this hypocrisy that I have personally witnessed is the church's ability to benefit from the talents or gifts of the LGBTQ community while at the same time condemning or pretending not to be aware of their sexual orientation. This selective ignorance is evident by the number of gay individuals who sing, play music, or contribute to the church's services in some capacity. Because of their vulnerability, youth are often victimized by church leadership, both physically and sexually. Frequently, when this abuse occurs early enough in a child's development, the child might identify with the energy of the same sex abuser and continue the lifestyle throughout their life even though it was not their initial choice. I have met many men who struggle with their sexual identity into adulthood due to molestation in their youth.

Suicide

Suicide is the second leading cause of death for our young people between the ages of 10-24. LGBTQ youth contemplate suicide at a rate of three times the rate of their heterosexual peers and are five times more likely to have made a suicide attempt. LGBTQ youth also represent 20-40% of all homeless young people in America. This rate is mostly attributed to being forced to leave their homes because their families' religious beliefs did not accept them, according to the National Gay and Lesbian Task Force Policy Institute. These youth often feel a conflict between accepting their religious beliefs and accepting their sexual identity. An Austrian study concluded that religion could at once be both a risk and a protective factor against suicidality in religiously affiliated sexual minority individuals. Many youths fear the possibility of going to hell if they commit suicide. Still, several studies have shown that the fear of hell often is not enough of a deterrent to prevent these troubled youth from making the ultimate escape from their sad reality.

I told you the facts, now let me give you the real about suicide. I was blessed enough to have suffered the hopelessness of being suicidal. I say blessed because it is challenging to try to help someone in the throes of the pain and torment that leads you to the point of apparent no return if you haven't experienced it yourself. The gutter truth is that suicide happens when the idea of living another day is more intolerable than taking your chances of seeing what is on the other side. It is a point where you feel like it is not worth trying to face another day of pain, failure, and disappointment. Leaving it all behind is a seductive siren that woos you to enter the depths of her nothingness. ***The problem with this prospect is that in most cases, the enigma with suicide is not so much that you want to die but that you have no idea how to live anymore in your present condition.*** The thought of suicide is like an abysmal falling into oblivion that offers no way to freedom from its clutches. It is an almost poetic place of existence to be quite honest. If the illusion that suicide offers were not so inviting, no one would do it.

The truth that suicide's enchantment doesn't allow you to realize is that wherever you are right now is NOT where you have to remain. Even in your lowest point of pain and low self-esteem, you still have the essence of the Creator within yourself. There are possibilities—unlimited possibilities. You have a universal paintbrush that can erase your current condition and create a portrait that leads to beauty and serenity. You only have to pick it up and paint it. You won't find this brush in a church or synagogue even though you think that you can only allow yourself to see it there. But your truth is that at any moment, you can change the reality in which you live. In short, "Suicide is a permanent solution to a temporary problem."

If you feel persecuted for your sexual orientation, find like-minded individuals who share your experience either in person or online. Today, both secular and some religious organizations have programs for the LGBTQ community. For the spirit of suicide to be successful, she requires isolation to do her work. The key is to reach out beyond yourself to realize the power that is already inside of you. You are not alone; some people care. Your journey may require that you cut ties with friends or family that do not approve of your lifestyle decisions. It may be unfortunate, but it is possible to find connections to other people who can become a surrogate family to you. Your existence is only to live your soul's truth, not to fulfill another person's perception of who you should or could be. Love them anyway. Thank them for the time you had with them. Move on towards your truth. You cannot choose your birth family, but you do get to choose your extended surrogate family. Lucky you!

But I Love Church Though

Okay, so you hear everything I have shared with you, but you still desire the comfort of a religious organization. I felt that it would be only fair to share some alternatives since I did mention the traditional religions in this book. No worries, you are most certainly not alone. The Methodist church has an extension called the Reconciling Ministries Network. It is an up and coming group that teaches inclusion for those who desire to worship within the Methodist community. There is the UCC Coalition for LGBT Concerns, UU Welcome and Equality, and the Unitarian Universalists congregations of which I am a member. Dignity USA is a Roman Catholic alternative for those of the Catholic faith. The Gay Christian Network is a group of people who have united to worship within the Christian faith. Integrity USA supports Episcopalian teaching. Keshet is for those who follow Judaism, and Lutherans Concerned North America/ Reconciling works is also an alternative.

Remember, you do not need any church organization to validate your worth or your place in the universe. God already accepts you because you are its creation. If God had intended for there to be no gay individuals, He is smart enough to have left homosexuality out the picture as an option or possibility. If there can be same-sex interactions in the animal kingdom and animals with dual sexuality, then isn't it within the realm of chance that you as a human being may not be a mistake at all? Your purpose here in this time of living the best expression of you that your soul desires. Be who and what you choose to be. Apologize to no one for who you are.

Next Steps and Takeaways from this chapter:

The Debate: Is sexuality something that anyone can choose at any point in their life, or is it static and predesigned at birth?

As in other chapters, I advocate that you assess your religion of choice. Are you following a religious system that serves your highest sense of self? Are you in a place that allows you to grow and to flourish in your freedom? Are you complying with specific rules or regulations with which you do not agree just to belong to a familial or social network? If so, are there other places that would allow you to be who you are in truth and strengthen your spiritual development? You can live in a place of denial. But that denial will only afford you a life of pain and struggle.

One reason we see such a large spectrum of self-identification through binary and non-binary terms is because we are starting to realize our beingness. There are so many ways your soul may choose to just "be." There is so much freedom of expression available to you within the universe. You need only choose the expression that serves your highest self. These identities are nothing new. Remember "there is nothing new under the sun."

You cannot be happy if you are not fulfilling your soul's purpose. I don't care how successful you become or how much money you make. For this reason, you see so many wealthy, successful, celebrity, and other accomplished people commit suicide. They are living a life that is incongruent with their true self. There is no way around it, unfortunately. You owe it to yourself to live your truth and avoid the pain to yourself and others around you that can be adversely affected by your decisions.

Meet Merin in his own words:

As a Lutheran, confirmation was a really big deal for me. I loved all of the hymns, the prayers, and the fellowship during the worship services. Receiving the Eucharist during holy communion is always a special time for me because I feel closer to God. I think I was different from a lot of my friends who really didn't want to have to go to church sometimes.

I have often wondered about other religions like Hinduism, Islam, or Buddhists. Can all of these other religions be wrong since they are so different from what I grew up with? Does God hear their prayers? They have so many people around the world who follow those religions. So it makes you wonder why things are so different for other people.

But even though I have had my questions, I will always be a Christian. Nothing can deter me from my faith in Jesus Christ our Lord and Savior. It feels good when I go to church and I see all of the statues and pictures on the stained-glass windows. It feels so real and so comforting to me.

I think at the end of the day, it all boils down to faith. I have faith in God and nothing can ever change my mind. But I do believe that God is a part of other religions as well. And everyone has to follow their heart as to which religion is the right one for them. The only people I do not understand are the ones that say there is no God whatsoever. How can you deny all of the beautiful things in creation? All of these things could not have just come from nowhere. I see God in the water and in the mountains. Only God can explain all of the beauty in the world.

If I had the opportunity to talk with an atheist, I would try to share with them the love that God has put in me. Maybe then they could see things another way. That's all I have to say.

CHAPTER 13 CONNECTING WITH THE UNIVERSE

> *"True religion comes not from the teaching of men or the reading of books; it is the awakening of the spirit within us, consequent upon pure and heroic action." Swami Vivekananda*

Understand that we are all God, God is in all of us, and God is everywhere. As a creator, God has imparted this vital gift and ability to create into every one of us. Let me share this experience. When I was around 15 years old, I went on a trip to Washington, DC, with a youth program that I participated in as an extracurricular activity. A friend and I were walking and exploring the monuments and all of the history there. As we walked across the massive square near the Lincoln Memorial, we passed a homeless man lying in the middle of the square. I vividly remember that I was eating a bag of pork rinds as we walked upon him. I told my friend he may be hungry, so I laid my bag of chips on his chest. My thought was that he might eat them when he awoke sometime later on.

As we walked a few steps away from him, I instinctively turned around to see if he had stirred and had seen the chips. To our disbelief, he had disappeared! The square is flat, and there was no way that he could have walked away without seeing him. It was impossible not to have seen him. We turned around in amazement in circles as though somehow, he could have raced past us without seeing him. Nevertheless, he was nowhere to be seen. I would ponder about this event for years to come. Had I seen an angel? Some might suggest he was an alien.

Perhaps we were seeing someone from another dimension. To this day, I cannot say definitively. But what I do know is that I did not hallucinate, unless there is such a thing as double hallucination! I was not alone, and we both witnessed the very same thing at the very same time. As I would later recount this occurrence to friends, I would always say that I have seen an angel. I always felt like my life was blessed after that moment because of my kindness to a stranger. I always sensed a presence watching over me and protecting me from the bad things in life and, at times, from myself.

I think the moral of the story is that there are many things in the universe that we cannot explain. We hear accounts of alien interactions, mythical and mystical being sightings, paranormal experiences, and the like. So, it seems clear to me that the universe desires to interact with us on some level. I am in no position to judge or invalidate another's experience when I have so clearly had my own. In this segment of my book, we will look at ways to engage with the universe proactively since I cannot recreate my personal experience with the angel. And I feel relatively safe that most others cannot recreate their own similar experiences at will. Is that fair? And as the number of ways to connect to the universe is innumerable, I will only focus on a few prospects here. And if you thought you were going to get a regurgitation of every other spiritual book on this subject, you will be pleasantly surprised.

Prophesy

All of my life, I have witnessed those who present themselves as prophets. According to Wikipedia, a prophecy is a message claimed by a prophet to have been communicated to them by a deity. Such messages typically involve inspiration, interpretation, or revelation of the divine will concerning the Prophet's social world and events to come. I like the use of the word "deity" because it does not predicate who or what the spiritual being is. There are notable Prophets throughout histories such as Moses, Nostradamus, Muhammad, and a host of others across spiritual planes. It begs the question of whether or not a person can reveal the past, present, or future to us via telepathic means?

The answer is yes. The Universal mind knows everything, and all of that knowledge is available now. There is no other time that exists beyond the eternal now in which we all live. Tomorrow never comes, and it was never yesterday. Everything that is happening now, what will happen, or has occurred in the past is now available. To grasp this concept, we must understand that we are all connected to the universal subconscious mind, which is God. This divine connection gives us entrée into all of the knowledge of the universe. Those who can tap into this resource can gain insight into that which is, has been, and potentially will be.

I think it is important to note that the future is not yet written. When a prophet looks into the universe, they look into the abyss of possibilities when they suggest what might happen in the future. What will transpire will ultimately depend on the law of attraction that manifests in that space in time. I can recall Prophet Roy Taylor (deceased) telling my friend who had been declared barren by her physicians that she would have a baby within one year. At the time, her husband was over 70 years old, and she was in her 30's. I can recall thinking that it would be fascinating to see if that extrapolation of prophecy could ever come true. In my mind, this kind of divination was quite specific, presumptuous, and highly unlikely to occur.

Most importantly, if the prediction did not come true, it would reflect very negatively against the Prophet. Yet within one year, to everyone's shock and amazement, baby Olivia was born. How was this man able to look into the impossible and predict an unimaginable event? On another occasion, Prophet Taylor called me up to the front of the church. He admonished me to get rid of the gun I had in my possession hidden underneath my truck's seat. I was shocked because absolutely no one knew that I had the gun. I had purchased it from a crackhead for $25.00. Needless to say, this was a man for whom I had much respect, as did others who would come from miles away to hear what he had to say from God.

I use this example because I experienced this man personally. But I also possessed and used the gift fluently once upon a time. In what I have to describe as a trance-like state, I could look into the universe and see inside your home. Or I could tell you things about yourself that I had no way of knowing. I stopped using my gift because I associate my gift to the church and religion. And since I had left the church, I left my gifts behind as well. At the time, I did not understand that my gift was not attached to any religious origins. I still have "flashes" of intuition that come through and are as spontaneous as getting the hiccups.

We all have inherent abilities to tap into the universe by various degrees throughout our lifetime. Sometimes we may call it a hunch, or "I had a feeling," or most commonly, "something told me..." Somehow my mother always knew when I was getting into trouble, and it made me feel like she could always see over my shoulder. I used to have psychic dreams that would awaken me from my sleep. These dreams would show me something negative that was going on in my life that I should be aware of so that they would not blindside me with 100% accuracy. In the secular world, we refer to people who demonstrate such gifts as psychics. We are all pure energy, and those that pay attention can pick up and decipher the energy emitted from others. This is why some say that they communicate with the dead and seem to share remarkable details about the departed's life to the listener's astonishment. The knowledge of their lives and all things of the past is in the universal subconscious and is available to anyone who seeks to learn from it.

Make no mistake, there are charlatans and those who prey upon the hurting, desperate, and vulnerable with trickery and deceit. I would take any readings, prophecies, or predictions with a grain of salt and discern whether they resonate with my soul. But no matter how credible the Prophet or psychic might be, your future is in your own hands. Whatever possibility that they may present to you for the future is only a possibility. You have the final say as to whether or not you accept or reject their adumbration. This is why it may sometimes seem that a true prophet or psychic is fake when a prediction fails to come true. They should always preface any prediction that any knowledge shared is not absolute but merely an opportunity in the universe. Remember that you are a part of the universe. That connection gives you power over your outcomes, no matter the prognostication.

Meditation

In my opinion, meditation is one of the easiest ways to engage with the universal subconscious mind. Meditation is a practice where an individual uses a technique – such as mindfulness or focusing the mind on a particular object, thought, or activity – to train attention and awareness, and achieve a mentally clear and emotionally calm and stable state. Meditation allows one to quiet the noise of the conscious mind and control thought, anxiety, stress, fear, or any undesirable emotion one might be experiencing. This practice teaches one to observe rather than participate in conscious thought. When I first began learning about meditation, I often found it challenging to focus my mind and thoughts. Today, I can immediately calm myself from any form of angst by centering myself and focusing on my breathing to deescalate my mind from potential stress or anxiety.

The stark reality here is that in America, anxiety disorders are the leading cause of mental illness with nearly 40,000,000 sufferers, according to the Anxiety and Depression Association of America. I had developed severe anxiety and PTSD due to many horrific, violent relationships, car wrecks, and abuse. Alcoholism only exacerbated my anxiety. I would startle at the slightest stimulus and would visibly shake when surprised. Add panic attacks and chronic insomnia to the mix, and you have the makings for a very bleak existence. Today in my serenity, meditation has become a tool that I can deploy at the ready whenever I am faced with stress or a situation that can create anxiety for me. I cannot imagine having to live once again in the prison of fear, which is why I feel that my soul must share this magnificent instrument of peace with others.

Music

One of the most precious and most powerful gifts that you have in the human realm is the ability to create and appreciate music. In 1697, William Congreve gave us the following poem from The Mourning Bride:

"Musick has Charms to sooth a savage Breast, To
soften Rocks, or bend a knotted Oak."

Although we commonly have replaced the term breast with the word beast, the gist of the message is relatively the same. Music has the power to evoke a myriad of human emotions in the listener. The mere fact that music can impact human emotion, which controlled by the soul, music can be a spiritual medium. When an individual becomes entranced by the flow or melody of music, the listener can experience a euphoric sensation. I have certain songs that I love to listen to when I am upset that instantly make me feel better. Lovers have that particular song that they listen to repeatedly while in the throes of heartbreak. The sad melody song at a funeral can move the entire crowd to tears. Hearing the star bangled banner song by an amazing singer can evoke a strong feeling of patriotism. Certain songs can rile the crowd at a concert into a frenzy of energy, anger, or even recklessness. Love songs can get you in the mood for love-making.

It is no wonder that most religions have some form of music incorporated into their worship, rituals, and practices. Music can have a hypnotic effect that can drive listeners into a more pliable and suggestable state. Most alter calls within Christian churches always have the musicians to play soft, slow, sad music that seduces the crowd to want to come and turn their lives over to God. Praise music seems to get the audience excited, while worship music is meant to create a sense of solemnness and reverence for their God's presence in the sanctuary.

Dancing

Oh My God! I could not even let myself off the hook and not put in one of the most freeing expressions of spirituality that I ever experience by myself (or with others). There is absolutely nothing with the absolute power and ability to shake loose any negative energy that has shackled my very spirit than the abandonment of being lost in the dance. It doesn't matter if you have the latest moves because it doesn't matter who sees you. Dance is the body's ability to commune with the universe in a way that requires no language. Dance allows pure unadulterated expression of any emotion that you may be feeling. It is no surprise that you find so much electric energy in a club where the music is jumping, and the crowd is on the floor doing their thing. There are a collective consciousness and spiritual bonding that occurs when you hear a song like "The Electric Slide," no matter what race, creed, or color that you are.

I have seen people dance this dance in unity who spoke different languages. This dance was able to bring them together in a way that words would never be able to do. Dancing provides a spiritual conduit connecting you with others. There are heat and fire that breaks forth from the burst of energy when you dance that is amazing. When you couple dance with the right music, you have countless opportunities to allow your soul to sing in live motion without a voice. Dance can be a form of therapy that frees you from inhibitions that keep you in stagnation or a helpless place.

In the church, you can see the people who "feel the spirit" break forth in what they call a holy dance. The tribes in Africa tell stories and ancestral histories in the form of dance. The native Americans perform many rituals in the form of dance. Almost every society and culture have some kind of celebration and expression that is displayed through dance. This is for a good reason. When you are dancing, you are free to be in the moment.

Prayer

A common idea of prayer suggests beseeching a divine being for permission, assistance, or guidance with the outcome to be decided at the mercy of whatever being you choose to ask. This idea goes back to the notion of God being a Supreme Being who is sitting in the great beyond somewhere, or in some cases, physically in your home or place of worship. This Being is just waiting around to answer your requests or to dole out punishments at its leisure. Again, you are not separate from God. If you feel the need to leverage the practice of prayer, you should understand that you are talking to the God within yourself.

The idea of prayer for favors provides a false sense of comfort that is not necessary to achieve your desired goals. God put each of us here to experience this existence, and you get to decide what those encounters will entail for you individually. The problem comes when you attempt to use prayer to control, impact, or alter another's behavior. Prayer as a request for help is a tool that provides you with a false sense of control over an event's outcome. You pray that he gets better. You pray that she will love you. You pray that you get the job. You pray that you will get the money that you need. There are thousands of examples that I could list here. Do you think that God has to weigh in on every decision that you make?

There is no God that is haphazardly making bad things happen to good people or making wonderful things happen to bad people. God is the source from which you can create the reality of your choosing. The universe is here to bring forth the things that you create through your thoughts into the physical world.

For over a year, I focused on how my old director was out to get me. And guess what? She got me. Through the Law of Attraction, I manifested my demise by concentrating on it, telling anyone who would listen about it, and worrying to the point of giving energy and life to the very thing that I did NOT want to happen. The devil didn't do it. God didn't let or make it happen. I created it—me, me, me, me, me, me, me.

The truth is that you do not have power or control over others. There is no prayer that you can say to change this fact. You cannot "pray" your child off of drugs. You cannot pray your husband into being faithful. In truth, when you pray for things to happen, you only have a 50/50 chance of the prayer coming true —you might as well flip a coin. So instead, why not focus on keeping your thoughts on the things you want to see happening for yourself in all situations. Likewise, people only change when they desire to do so. Praying for them to control them is a wasted energy practice.

If you must pray, let your prayer state your positive or desired intentions for yourself into the universe. Focus your energies towards the thoughts that serve your highest good. Use prayer as a means of reinforcing your highest dreams and strengths. Before you go into a meeting, state your intentions to the universe like so:

> In this meeting, I intend to communicate my ideas in a thoughtful and meaningful way. Together we will find a resolution to all of our concerns that will benefit all of those involved.
>
> Or
>
> I intend to send thoughts of love, joy, peace, and healing to my loved one. I surround them with my love and care and desire a speedy recovery for them during this time. And I support whatever outcome they want for themselves.

Prayer should only be a statement of your own intentions and desires. You can send positive thoughts and energy towards other individuals. But you cannot control others through the power of prayer. Would that not be a form of witchcraft? What happens in life is neither good nor bad; it just is. Prayer is not a weapon of control to manipulate the outcome of our lives. Being angry at God for a loss of a loved one or other event in our lives that you decide is unfavorable is an exercise in futility. Death is promised to everyone who lives—from this, there is no escape.

You must enjoy every moment of your existence and focus your energies on fulfilling your soul's desires. You cannot control others. You can try, but it does not work out well. Too much of life is wasted by praying for things to happen or not happen. Live your life in serenity, and that which serves your highest self instead. In prayer, you often state an intention for something you desire to attract but give the universe instruction on how to bring it to pass. The universe does not work that way. You can state your intention and be water. Flow in positive energy and allow the universe to guide you on the path to what you desire.

Additionally, you cannot use prayer to circumvent the Law of Cause and Effect. Remember, you cannot escape the universal laws. This is not to say that miracles cannot happen. But you cannot use manipulation to get them.

Collective Consciousness

In this new age of the COVID-19 pandemic, the "Me Too Movement" and Black Lives Matter, you see a universal shift in the ideas of how life should look in our society. Throughout history, you have seen similar shifts that appear to change how we have chosen to engage with each other in the world. Collective consciousness is the set of ideas, beliefs, and moral attitudes that are shared by a group in society. Because the universal mind responds to thoughts that spur creation, whenever a large group of people focuses on the same thought or idea, the collective energies become a force that can change society's entire dynamic. It is when these thoughts join collectively that enough momentum generates to create change on a massive scale.

We have the potential to create world peace or to end world hunger if we so choose. It would only depend on creating a source of collective consciousness that would allow such an effort to unfold. The only reason we have not done so is that powers that be do not sincerely wish it so. We have lived under the illusion of lack of abundance, limited resources, and selfishness. These views have provided the fuels that fan the fires of wars, hatred, and division. The truth is there is enough for everyone. The universe has perpetuated nothing but abundance, procreation, and sustenance for thousands of years. It is humanity who lives in breach of the harmony that the universe intended with inequities and uneven distributions of wealth and resources.

For the Millennials, this is YOUR time! It's your time to rage against the machine of religious machinations that have attempted to strangle your youth, voice, and critical thinking. Now is the time for you to define your own reality and speak for your generation—for the members of your time within this space of history—in a new voice. You can shout from the rooftops that you will be heard. You will be acknowledged. You will be free to explore your divinity, your morality, and your truth. Protest the hypocrisy of the older generations. Denounce racism, for it only serves to divide and to breed hatred. Picket the religious establishment that bans independent thought and the real search for knowledge and truth. A collective consciousness of freedom is yours to manufacture and implement the changes you want to see in our world tomorrow. If you fail to learn from our history, you are doomed to repeat it.

Next Steps and Takeaways from this chapter:

The Debate: Should you pray for a dying loved one if it is against their will to live?

Your purpose for being is to experience the world in whatever way you desire. I know this to be so because the experience is the only thing that you genuinely have that cannot be taken away in this lifetime. Material things come and go. Even Jesus said in Matthew 19-21:

> *"Do not store up for yourselves treasures on earth, where moths and vermin destroy, and where thieves break in and steal. But store up for yourselves treasures in heaven, where moths and vermin do not des troy, and where thieves do not break in and steal. For where your treasure is, there your heart will be also."*

These treasures are the joys that you experience through living the life your soul aspires to live. The earthly materials that you may gain and enjoy are not the end but the means. You acquire riches on earth because you serve others—goods exchanged for service. If you want to increase our wealth and prosperity, increase your service. Your service should be sharing with the world the fruits of your highest self. In summary, your connection to the universal mind is your entrée into the world of creation. The thoughts that you give energy create the reality that you experience. If you want to change your existence, change your thoughts. This is why the wise Solomon said in Proverbs 23:7, "As he thinketh in his heart, so is he." The universe only responds to thought, so it is incumbent upon us to be intentional about the thoughts that we give energy. Instead of worrying or focusing on what we do not want, focus only on what you want to see happen in your life through all of the various means we have to connect with the universe.

Meet The Recoverist in her own words:

I have talked about how I grew in a very religious home. I came from four generations of pastors. I was supposed to marry a Bishop or someone else in high authority within the church. But my life didn't take that path. I studied various religions at great length to find out that the God I was looking for is already inside of me because I am God. Through personal experience, I have come to know that I am a part of Pure Spirit and everyone else in the world.

I have learned that I cannot live by other people's expectations of what is right for me. My truth is that I am everything that I want to be now and whoever I choose to be tomorrow. My mission is to fulfill my soul's desire "to be." That "being" consists of giving love and spiritual freedom to anyone who wishes to discover their truth and to unburden themselves from the chains of unrealistic expectations. I am a deliverer of them who are bound.

CHAPTER 14 SURVIVING YOUR CRUCIBLE

> *"The greatest religion is to be true to your own nature. Have faith in yourselves."* Swami Vivekananda

Before we delve into surviving your crucible, let's first understand what I mean as I contemplate this powerful statement. A crucible is a severe, searching test or trial. For any of you who are either lost in the sea of depression, or trapped within the frays of addiction, or to those of you in the process of breaking free of the confines of religious beliefs that don't quite mesh with what your soul is telling you this is a critical point in your quest for truth. Remember that every moment of your life is a coin toss of infinite possibilities. You can change your destiny with every new decision. Nothing is permanent save death and your soul's departure from your mortal body.

It's Your Choice

Whatever path you choose, and I repeat you choose, for yourself can be a wonderfully fulfilling experience. You are God's expression of Himself (as you), and the path that you choose is pleasing to God no matter what it may be—there are no mistakes. You are born into this world alone, and you will die alone. And one of the most precious gifts that you will receive when you enter this physical plane is the gift of choice. No matter what you have chosen for yourself up until this point in your life, your course is something that you can change whenever you desire to do so. It doesn't matter if you are in jail, in active addiction, in an unhappy or unhealthy relationship, homeless, or any undesirable condition you can fathom. You can change it at any moment by changing your perception and perspective of what you want your future to be.

The world is yours, and the only limits are those that you manufacture in your own mind. You owe it to yourself to get to know your soul. You do not want to live a one-dimensional life with a total focus on your body or material things. And you should equally desire to expand beyond the two-dimensional existence of the body and the body-mind only focusing on the day-to-day mundaneness of just keeping things going or barely getting by. Or even doing well financially like I was, but dying daily from the pain of living up to someone else's standards, you can never possibly measure up. They will always want more. My corporation raised our company goals every year, and each goal was more impossible than the one we barely got close to the year before. You are a three-fold being, and your spirit should always be considered when making choices for your life.

Do not limit yourself to loveless relationships that meet others' approval or fulfill obligations that bring a false sense of security. Let your soul guide the way to loving yourself so very much that you attract the soul that loves you equally and freely. Forego the need of love for the practice of being love through the demonstration of every act you lovingly share with the world. Allow yourself to embrace the glorious lovemaking that brings you to the height of spiritual ecstasy with abandon and freedom. Permit yourself to enjoy all of the exquisiteness of joining with a kindred soul with a love that can flourish.

Guilt and shame are constructs designed by man to make you feel wrong about who and what you indeed are. Decide to fully love yourself and other people understanding that true love cannot harm another because, in doing so, you would be hurting yourself. In love, show forgiveness for perceived wrongs from others. Show compassion for those who are against you, knowing that they are a part of you. Unburden your soul of past hurts and disappointments by flailing your energy towards a positive and productive future instead.

Choose to let go of any programming that has penetrated your subconscious mind with seeds of poison, lies, and falsehoods about who you are and who you can be. You are God, and you are everything, and the world is your oyster. They say that what doesn't kill you only makes you stronger. I disagree. I believe that the truth that you deny yourself about who you are can kill you, and to seek your truth makes you stronger. People have been taught by others who taught them to manipulate and control with words that breed fear and insecurity in the hearer's ear. You have the power to silence that noise.

God would not create you the way that you are if the way that you are is wrong. She would not form in you the desires, hopes, and dreams that you possess only to deny you the knowledge of those desires, hopes, and dreams. How cruel would that be? It would be like creating a flower and demanding it not to bloom. Or creating a caterpillar and forbidding it to enjoy the rapture of becoming a beautiful butterfly. What would be the point of creating billions of people who are all sinners and on their way to hell? How weak would a God have to be to fail at his own creation billions of times for an eternity? And then because of his failure, punish every one of his creation for his own error. This prospect is unfathomable for me. And if it were true, I would not worship that God anyway.

As you traverse your crucible, I would offer that you think of this searching in a much similar fashion to the lovely Marie Kondo. If you don't know who she is, she is who I will affectionately refer to as the "does it bring you joy, lady." She is an expert on how to remove clutter from your life and your home. She admonishes her followers to pick up an item and observe whether or not this particular item brings its owner joy. If it does not, she recommends that you thank it for its service and politely put it away and out of your life. With this reference in mind, if you attend religious services, ask yourself, does this service or spiritual practice bring you joy?

Manage Your Stinkin' Thinkin'

I would like to introduce a concept to you here about how you "think." If you take nothing else away from this book, please take this idea away. The more aware that you are about the fact that thoughts come from the universe in many forms and in many ways that may or may not make sense, the better off you will be. Be aware of the next time some random thought "pops" into your head and know that you do not have to entertain it because it came into your awareness. Do not allow people or situations to rent space in your head for free. Any thoughts that you entertain should be those that fulfill you, improve you, and exemplify your highest good. Remember that ideas are the seeds of creation. If you do not want to see it manifest into your reality, let that thought go on its merry way. In time, you will train yourself to guard your thoughts and manage those thoughts to your highest good.

Give me that Ol' Time Religion (It's good enough for me)

And if at the end of your crucible, you decide that you need religion with its comforts, social involvement, and fellowship, if religion serves your soul, then continue in your faith. I only caution you to do so from a place of freedom fully embracing your power of self. There is absolutely nothing wrong with deciding to continue your Jewish tradition, attending your Catholic Mass, or meditating at your temple. The point is that you are free to do so without impunity! Well, you might ask, if I know my truth, is it inauthentic to still attend a religious ceremony when I do not believe the extent of their teachings? I would tell you it is not inauthentic. Your soul is free to experience whatever it desires. You can go to Mass and then go to the Buddhist temple on the same day if you choose to do so.

It is about expressing your freedom of choice and not acting out of addiction or fear. It's about not doing something because you feel obligated, guilted, or shamed into doing so. I no longer attend church regularly, as I find it unnecessary for my spiritual life. However, I appreciate most of what the Bible purports Jesus to have taught. But in the same breath, I also know that the translations of what we call the Bible has been stepped on more times than a bag of heroin on the streets of Detroit. A group of men decided which texts should be included, and more importantly, which books would be excluded from the Bible. I do not need a bible or holy book to tell me who I am. But I can learn and develop my highest self while including the findings in sacred texts that ring true for my soul into my sense of soul identity.

What's it all about?

Your crucible is about your soul undergoing the process of realizing its potential during this lifetime. The end of your journey is physical death, and there is no escape from this end for anyone. Death is not to be feared, for everyone will encounter death at some point. Your physical death is the moment in which your soul decides to end this experience. Many souls stay longer in this plane because they have loved ones who wish it so. Others fulfill a brief sojourn in this realm and go back to the universe from which it came. As someone once said, what matters is what happens in the "dash"—the time between your birth date and your death date. Your job is to enjoy the dash to the fullest. Not at the expense of harming others, but at the cost of challenging yourself to create the best experience you can for yourself while you are here. Cherishing every moment and soaking up the joy, excitement, and glory of the freedom of just "being." We are humans "being," not humans trying or humans surviving—humans being.

What about Morality?

It is your job to define your own moral code. As I mentioned earlier, your morality will evolve over your lifetime. It may develop from moment to moment. Your parents do the best that they can to instill their value system into you as their child. How do you decide what pieces of their values are relevant to your reality? If your parents were racists, how do you choose to include those values or reject those values into your moral code? Your soul will tell you. If you take this time to review the values you hold and allow yourself to judge each value and observe how you feel about it from the depths of your soul, you will sense a feeling of joy or sorrow. You cannot convince, cajole, or deceive your soul into believing something your spirit knows to be uncomfortable or untrue. You can try to mislead others into thinking that you think a thing just to fit in with them. But when you are alone with yourself, you know the truth you hold.

Love and Tolerance

Love and tolerance are the cure for the addiction of religion. Only you have governance over your soul. You don't get to have governance over anyone else's soul. This includes your children, your spouse or partner, and your friends and family. Every soul has to complete its own journey. Part of the problems in the entire world surrounds one person or one group errantly usurping authority over another person's thoughts, actions, and, ultimately, their well-being. The Law of Allowing, as described by Abraham Hicks, suggests the following: I am who I am, and you are who you are. In other words, I respect your right to be who you are while at the same time accepting that who you are does not impede my ability to be who I am. I may not choose to worship your God with you but refrain from making a judgment against you for doing so. And likewise, I acknowledge your right to do the same for me. When it was all said and done, at the end of my crucible, I found out that I am love, and I will give love in the way that my soul has chosen to do so—by helping you.

Next Steps and Takeaways from this chapter:

The Debate: Can everyone have their own sense of morality and

sense of personal religion or life code?

You might note that there are no more stories. From here, you share your own and begin the journey to write the rules of your soul's religion. What serves your soul's sense of the highest self? What is your personal morality? What ideas will you discard, and conversely, what pieces will you keep? Look in the mirror, and there you find everything that you need for success in this world. I have heard this kind of language before and never understood it. "Everything I need is in me." What the hell does that even mean? I hope that at the end of this journey, you now have a sense of the right questions to ask to start your quest for enlightenment. And by enlightenment, I mean to personify the word's true definition: Greater knowledge and understanding of a subject or situation. In this case, the situation is your soul's journey.

You know, the thing that if money were no object and you could do it all day every day, this would be your dream. You owe it to yourself to start the deprogramming of undesirable thinking and begin creating your own identity and sense of self.

CHAPTER 15 MY FAVORITE MEDITATION STYLES

Nature is my temple; trees are my priests; birds, my rabbis; rains, my imams! Nature is my only true and eternal religion."
Mehmet Murat Ildan

I did not want to stir up all of this longing to experience the splendor of the universe for yourself and fail to give you a decent start to your journey. I enjoy meditations because they help you channel your inner strength in a way that allows you to bypass your egocentric consciousness and tap into the universal subconscious's infinity. Many people have settled for prayer alone, which has been grossly misused for selfish purposes. Beseeching God as though she were a fairy godmother is a trite expenditure of your valuable time. Alignment with the universe's vibrations gives you control of how you choose to engage with space and time, which is a better use of your time. Declaring your intentions and stating them with faith and hope are the genuine opportunities to impact your existence.

In this chapter, I am sharing some of the effortless and efficient methods of meditation that I have found helpful in my daily practice and in times of anxiety, fear, and indecision. Throughout this book, I have plied you with glimpses of my story and my journey to finding my truth. I have run the gamut of existence. I was born, I have lived, and I have died. Yet my soul chose to stay here in this world a little while longer. I am here to share my discoveries with all of you. But the longing of my soul is to impart my experiences with the one who is still on his journey to the truth. Perhaps the sharing of my struggle to shed the confines of man's addiction to religion and walk in the freedom of oneness with the universe will help ease your transition to independence.

"If you are depressed, you are living in the past. If you are anxious, you are living in the future. If you are at peace, you are living in the present." Lao Tzu

I was ready to go into eternal rest that fateful day in the boardroom in Guadalajara, Mexico. But my soul said not yet. I agreed to allow my soul to complete its mission with certain expectations and demands from God in return. They have yet to make good on their part of the bargain, but if you are reading this book, I suspect they are willing to pay indeed. Maybe I will explain what that means in my next book. But for now, I am listing four styles of meditation that I include in my regimen. They are listed by increasing experience so that you can begin with something simple if you would like and give you different styles to choose from depending on your comfort level.

Coming into your truth requires that you shed all of the preconceived notions of certainty that you have digested from others. Demand from the universe that you experience its awesomeness and realize your power to walk in it as God, as creator, as a spectator, and as a whole part of its entirety without which you would be incomplete. Stand tall in your knowingness that you are a unique and critical thread in the universe's fabric. You are weaving the patterns of your experiences into the cloth of the eternal.

Revel in the opportunity to thrive and live in a world that would convince you that you are powerless and that you rely on its acceptance to be whole. You are irreplaceable, and the depths of the impact that you alone can leave upon the world is limited only to the heights of your imagination. The world is your oyster, your playground, and your pallet to paint your chosen picture upon its canvas. You are everything and nothing while also possessing a bounty of ideas and gifts to share with the world. I AM. I AM. I AM whatever I choose to be. They told me that "if you fail to go with-in, you will go with-out." Now let that marinate as we move forward.

Method One: Guided Meditation

Guided meditations typically have a narrator that guides you through the meditation with either word, instructions on breathing, or a chant. These are very helpful for those who are new to meditation and have not yet mastered the ability to still the body-mind. This is my absolute favorite guided meditation, and it comes from the book Three Magic Words by Uell. S. Anderson. This book is in my recommended reading list, and it has a meditation included at the end of each chapter. Three Magic Words is a compelling read. I recommend listening to the meditation below on YouTube, as led by Wayne Dyer. It plays the meditation over and over for about an hour. I would propose listening to it every morning and again at bedtime. You can also just listen to it while you do whatever. I like to read it aloud with Wayne, and I try to read this meditation before I go into any stressful situation. It serves me as a constant reminder of who I am and that I need not worry about anything.

"I know that I am pure spirit, that I always have been, and that I always will be.

There is inside me a place of confidence and quietness and security where all things are known and understood.

This is the Universal Mind, God, of which I am a part and which responds to me as I ask of it.

This universal mind knows the answer to all of my problems, and even now the answers are speeding their way to me.

I needn't struggle for them; I needn't worry or strive for them. When the time comes, the answers will be there.

I give my problems to the great mind of God; I let go of them, confident that the correct answers will return to me when they are needed.

Through the great law of attraction, everything in life that I need for my work and fulfillment will come to me.

It is not necessary that I strain about this, only believe. For in the strength of my belief, my faith will make it so.

I see the hand of divine intelligence all about me, in the flower, the tree, the brook, the meadow.
I know that the intelligence that created all these things is in me and around me and that I can call upon it for my slightest need.

I know that my body is a manifestation of pure spirit and that spirit is perfect; therefore, my body is perfect also.

I enjoy life, for each day brings a constant demonstration of the power and wonder of the universe and myself.

I am confident. I am serene. I am sure.

No matter what obstacle or undesirable circumstance crosses my path, I refuse to accept it, for it is nothing but illusion.

There can be no obstacle or undesirable circumstance to the mind of God, which is in me, and around me, and serves me now."

Here is another meditation, prayer, or poem that I find comforting and fantastic, so I wanted to share it with you. I first read in There is a Spiritual Solution to Every Problem by Wayne Dyer. I decided that the edicts listed here serve my soul's definition of being, and if it resonates with you, I welcome you to enjoy it as well. By Dr. Kent M. Keith and revised as Mother Teresa's Poem The Final Analysis:

People are often unreasonable, illogical, and self-centered; Forgive them anyway.

If you are kind, people may accuse you of selfish, ulterior motives; Be kind anyway.

If you are successful, you will win some false friends and some true enemies; Succeed anyway.

If you are honest and frank, people may cheat you; Be honest and frank anyway.

What you spend years building, someone may destroy overnight;

Build anyway.

If you find serenity and happiness, they may be jealous; Be happy anyway.

The good you do today, people will often forget tomorrow; Do good anyway.

Give the world the best you have, and it may never be enough; Give the world the best you've got anyway

You see, in the final analysis, it is all between you and God; It was never between you and them anyway.

I also enjoy affirmational guided meditations. I care for "I am," Gratitude, and Law of Attraction meditations. I recommend leveraging the thousands of guided meditations on YouTube for the various guided meditations they offer. You can use MeetUp, or similar apps, to locate the meditation groups in your area if you want to meet like-minded people and make new friends. Mindfulness is such a wondrous way to create serenity in your life and shut out the noise.

Method Two: Sound Meditation

I learned sound meditation from a Buddhist monk. I immediately fell in love with the activity. It was easy for me to grasp when I first got into meditation. I have a mind that used to race like a jackrabbit, and I often found it challenging to concentrate on meditation. The monk referred to the body-mind as a rabbit, and you have to distract the rabbit. The presence of sound gives the conscious mind something to focus on that will momentarily distract it from allowing random thoughts from infiltrating your meditation. You will soon learn how to observe your thoughts rather than allowing them to sidetrack you from your serenity, but in the meantime, sounds are very calming, relaxing, and helpful. There are many variations of sound meditation, such as repeating a mantra, using a Tibetan sound bowl, or using music to serve as the sound source. We all remember the Buddhist chant "Namu Myoho Renge Kyo" from Tina Turner's life movie "What's Love Got to do With it." The use of the Tibetan sound bowl offers the addition of vibration to your meditation experience, also called a sound bath.

The sound bowls are my favorite, and I train my clients to incorporate them into their meditation. Sound meditation also helps you learn how to tune out the background fray around you and focus on your inner stillness. The mind can be very tricky like the rabbit and may attempt to develop a dialogue about the sounds themselves. When this happens, gently rein your awareness inward to again focus on listening to the sound. Feel free to use your handy timer to keep time and continue to extend your sessions in five-minute increments until you reach a full hour. Your soul will thank you.

Method Three: Tapping (EFT)

Remember, I told you that I am open to everything and attached to nothing? Well, I first saw the custom of tapping on an episode of Iyanla Fix My Life on the OWN network. I thought that it was fascinating and decided to do some research on the subject. I include tapping in my meditation chapter because, uniquely, you are meditating and in communion with the universal subconscious. It could be the placebo effect, and even if it is, who cares if it works? Well, it did work. You can practice tapping to address several things like traumatic events, stress issues, or change negative thinking. It's super cool how tapping works, but what is also neat is that you can do it anywhere, anytime. They told me that I have arthritis (see how I don't claim it?).

This arthritis would cause aching in my joints despite the surgeries that I had to address the issues. To test this whole tapping phenomenon, I chose to tap for shoulder pain to leave my body. I only did the tapping for a couple of days, and now the aching in my shoulder is gone. When it tries to creep back up now and again, I simply tap it away, and it is gone. True story, and I am willing to take a lie detector test on that one! I have absolutely NO idea how or why it works. I just simply accept that it does. It's as if the act of tapping reprograms the neuroreceptors in your brain or something. So, enough preamble, let's get into tapping.

What is tapping? It is a combination of integrating Chinese acupuncture with affirmations. As Dr. Dawson Church says, "Acupoint tapping sends signals directly to the mid-brain stress centers, not mediated by the frontal lobes (the thinking part, active in talk therapy)." Because EFT simultaneously accesses stress on physical and emotional levels, he adds, "EFT gives you the best of both worlds, body, and mind, like getting a massage during a psychotherapy session." The basic technique requires you to focus on the negative emotion at hand: a fear or anxiety, a bad memory, an unresolved problem, or anything that's bothering you. While maintaining your mental focus on this issue, use your fingertips to tap 5-7 times each on 12 of the body's meridian points:

Abbreviations and anatomical references:

- **SS:** The Sore Spot - **Neuromyopathic point**
- **EB:** Beginning of the Eye Brow - **Bladder Meridian**
- **SE:** Side of the Eye - **Gall Bladder Meridian**
- **UE:** Under the Eye - **Stomach Meridian**
- **UN:** Under the Nose - **Governing Vessel**
- **Ch:** Chin - **Central Vessel**
- **CB:** Beginning of the Collar Bone - **Kidney Meridian**
- **BN:** Below Nipple - **Liver Meridian**
- **UA:** Under the Arm - **Spleen Meridian**
- **TH:** Top of the Head - **Governing Vessel**
- **Th:** Thumb- **Lung Meridian**
- **IF:** Index Finger - **Large Intestine Meridian**
- **MF:** Middle Finger - **Heart Protector**
- **BF:** Baby Finger - **Heart Meridian**
- **KC:** Karate Chop - **Small Intestine Meridian**

The practice of EFT is an alternative method of coping with both physical ailments and emotional distress by using a spiritual slant.

Method Four: Silent Meditation

Many of the people I work with complain that the body-mind is not cooperative when trying to attempt silent meditation. Their minds race, it is difficult to focus, and they try not to fidget. But picture being in outer space. There is nothing but silence. This is because in the center of the universe lies nothing but peace and nothingness. When you can calm your mind and tap into this quietness, you can connect to this stillness and raise your vibration to the highest level of positivity. In this place, you can make clear your intentions, and with your thought energy, you can bring into the physical world your deepest desires. Here you can release all of the stress, symptoms of burnout and connect with your soul.

Silent meditation can serve to improve your levels of concentration by teaching yourself to observe only your surroundings, your breathing, and your vibrations. You also enhance your spiritual connection with the universe while soothing your soul and increasing your compassion and sense of oneness with the world around you. In meditation, you learn to listen to your body and the inspiration you receive when you commune with the universal mind. They say that prayer is talking to God, but meditation is listening to God speak to you. In silence, you can achieve mental clarity and a calm mind.

It is effortless to begin your meditation at home. The first thing you want to do is set the mood for quiet, peace, and tranquility. I advocate having a dark room or space with candles for lighting, a comfortable pillow to sit upon, and a timer to let you know when you are done. When you are comfortably seated, set your timer for the desired length of time, you wish to meditate. I suggest 5 minutes to start, and then increase your time by 5-

minute augmentations when you feel that you are more comfortable with the silence and are willing to devote more time to your meditation. Either in your mind or aloud, state your intention for this meditation to the universe.

For example, I want to focus on releasing the stress from my body. Or, I will do well on this exam today. You can choose whatever energy that you desire to attract into your life. Take slow deep breaths and concentrate on breathing to inhale as deeply as possible, followed by as long an exhale that you can muster. Every time your mind begins to shift its focus away from your breath, and you get lost in thought, you gently bring your attention back to your breath. And then you repeat this again and again until your meditation timer rings.

Silent retreats can be beneficial for learning different techniques from those who specialize in yoga and meditation. When you have elevated your meditation skills, you can move up to spending designated blocks of time in silence. Dedicate one day per month to carve out time for complete silence. You will be amazed at how relaxed you feel when you unplug from all of the distractions of the phone, email, friends, or family. Remember that you can do even a few moments of this quiet exercise from anywhere: in the car before a stress ful event, before an exam to center yourself, or in a moment of anger, and you need to destress immediately. I have found that whenever I am in a moment of anxiety or extreme stress, I can calm myself by merely stilling my mind, closing my eyes, and taking deep breaths. It is similar to letting the air out of a balloon—the stress just slips away. In my mind, I may repeat a mantra like, "I am confident, I am serene, I am sure." It works, I promise! Stress comes from without, but your peace and serenity come from within. Own your serenity.

To sum up this chapter, there is NO one way or right way to experience meditation. You have to experiment and find the methods that work for you. I am encouraging you to be open to the possibility that if the ways you have been managing your anxiety have not been successful, meditation might be a way to help.

Next Steps and Takeaways from this chapter:

The Debate: Can you live your best life without meditation?

I have enjoyed going through this journey of The Addiction of Religion with you. I have grown so much as a result of the process of writing this book. I hope that I have raised questions, discussions, and debates that will challenge you as you embark upon your journey of "surviving your own crucible." No one is perfect by other people's standards, but you are perfect just the way you are because you are here—God's perfect creation of himself inside of you.

So, don't bother trying to reach enlightenment through someone else's path. Don't try to get "saved" to escape who you are. Heaven or hell is in the life you create right here on earth.

> *"Heaven in the sky is not a reward for righteous living. Heaven is the opportunity to experience the glory of living right here on earth; you have been beautifully given this time." K.D. Foy*

So, if you don't like what you see in your world, change it and create the life you want to live. "Be the change you want to see in the world," said Mother Theresa. As long as you breathe, the valuable part of God that gives your mortal body its animation shows that you still have time. You have all of the time in the world because the only time is now—the eternal now. Yesterday is gone. Tomorrow never comes. "All you ever really have is now" (to quote the illustrious J-lo on World of Dance).

My religion is living in alignment and harmony with myself and the universe. Your faith is the life code that you design to honor your own soul's "beingness." It is your way of existing in synchronization with universal source energy. Religion is your design and serves you as a living document and testament to your place in the world.

So, who is God? God is the following: Christianity, Mormonism,

Catholicism, animals, atheists, doctors, lawyers, gay, straight, plants, oceans, witchcraft, the universe, the beginning and the end, and everything in between. God is the energy that comprises and embodies all of creation. He is in all things, over all things, and the totality of all things. They are your smile, your pain, your success, and your failures. She is in every experience, every thought, and every pain. It is the good and the bad, the happy and the sad. "Through our eyes, the universe is perceiving itself.

Through our ears, the universe is listening to its harmonies. We are the witness through which the universe becomes conscious of its glory, of its magnificence." Alan Watts

You cannot throw a rock and miss the universe, for it is everywhere; it is even the rock in your hand. The only thing left for you to do is discover the God that is you and in you. God is here to do your bidding in the formation of whatever creation your heart desires to see in your reality. God is you. You are God. You are God, in part forever linked to your fellow man. We are like tiny slivers of God's giant pie in the sky. We are all one. So, love yourself, love your enemy, for she too is a part of you.

"God is all things, so there is no path that you can take that won't lead you to the universal mind." K. D. Foy

That is why I tell people that all religions are the correct path if they lead you to your highest self-awareness. There is the only choice, your choice, of how you choose to engage with universal source energy. Live your truth, walk out your journey, and order your steps.

"I enjoy a taste of Buddhism today, a sip of Christianity tomorrow. It is all available to me to experience as my soul sees fit. I have no boundaries and pledge no allegiance except to my soul." K.D. Foy

RECOMMENDED READING MATERIALS

As I told you at the preface of this book, I am open to everything but attached to nothing. I wanted to leave you with a few books to enhance your journey of soul exploration even further. I have read all of the books that I am recommending here and challenge you to be receptive to new concepts and ideas that might serve you from neoteric sources.

You are a Badass by Jen Sincero: This book was an unbelievable experience for me to read. She helped me to open up to new ideas about achieving my highest potential. She opened my mind to so many concepts, from vision boards to repairing your self-esteem. Her book is a down to earth (if you couldn't tell from the title!) approach to finding your place in the universe and living life to your fullest potential.

Three Magic Words by Uell S. Andersen is an eye-opening book of gigantic proportions. This book shares insight into the vast possibilities of humanity and the universe.

There's a Spiritual Solution to Every Problem by Wayne Dyer: Wayne Dyer is my hero. I wish I could have met him. He is such a source of inspiration for me on so many levels. He shares a plethora of knowledge on how to commune with the universe and live life to your highest potential.

Conversations with God Volumes 1-3 by Neale Donald Walsch: These books chronicle Neale's experiences with talking to God and having the conversations that answer the questions that we all wish we could have the opportunity to ask. Reading the answers to all of our problems from God's perspective is a unique opportunity to look at our world through a different lens.

EPILOGUE

My soul is filled with so much joy and serenity. It is my desire that you find the same. If this book can help you to initiate your own journey to your truth, then my soul is truly blessed. I cannot leave this work without acknowledging my sponsor, my mentor, and my spiritual guide The Great Don Bryan.

I am always interested to hear feedback from my readers as they examine these questions and debates. So, feel free to send your feedback to burningdesirespiritualrecovery@gmail.com. Or @burningdesirespiritualrecovery on IG. Namaste, and I love you, K. D. Foy

Please leave your review of this work on Amazon.com or whereever you were blessed to find this work.

ABOUT THE AUTHOR

K. D. Foy

The Recoverist was born in Detroit, MI. She presently lives in Atlanta, GA.

She was a single mother, Evangelist, Prophetess, International Call Center, Vendor Manager, Project Manager (PMP), and world traveler.

Then she became "No One" and "Everyone."

She is currently a member of Alcoholics Anonymous, a Reverend in the Universal Life Church. She has a Doctorate Degree in Theology.

Her life work is serving humanity as a Private One-On-One Personal Spiritual Drug and Alcohol Addiction Recoverist and Spiritual Life Coach. She is also the founder of Burning Desire Spiritual Recovery Services.

In preparation for this book, she refused all employment and lived by the rules of the Law of Attraction and other Universal laws for the space of one year in total reliance on the bounty of the Universe for sustenance and for the contents of this book.

This groundwork served to enable her to write a fully authentic account of her experiences. This book is what she calls her "soul's work." May it bless you.

www.ingramcontent.com/pod-product-compliance
Lightning Source LLC
Chambersburg PA
CBHW031132090426
42738CB00008B/1055
9781735630601